A HANDBOOK OF

PARISH MUSIC

A handbook of

PARISH
MUSIC

(REVISED EDITION)

A working guide for clergy and organists

by
LIONEL DAKERS

Director of the Royal School of Church Music

MOWBRAY
LONDON & OXFORD

© A. R. Mowbray & Co Ltd 1976, 1982

ISBN 0-264-66836-7

First published in 1976
This Revised Edition published 1982 by A. R. Mowbray & Co Ltd
Saint Thomas House, Becket Street, Oxford, OX1 1SJ

Typeset by Cotswold Typesetting Ltd, Cheltenham
and Printed in Great Britain by Biddles of Guildford

A cheerful spirit is the best convoy for religion. . . . Cheerfulness and a festival spirit fills the soul full of harmony, it composes music for churches and hearts, it makes and publishes glorification of God, it produces thankfulness and serves the ends of charity.

Jeremy Taylor
XXV Sermons

God grant me the serenity to accept things I cannot change, courage to change the things I can, and wisdom to know the difference.

Reinhold Niebuhr

Contents

Introduction

Much of this book is devoted to the *joint* work of the parson and organist, simply because in any ideal parochial situation worship and music must be envisaged as a joint occupation. Then, and only then, can the full impact of music in worship be realised. What the parson looks for in his organist, and *vice versa,* are vital to this concept, for the parson cannot wash his hands of the music and the musicians any more than the organist can view his work as merely music, full stop.

In the best situation, the one respects the specialised knowledge of the other and each seeks to further his work by benefiting from the particular expertise of his partner.

The parson and organist must work together as colleagues, never in isolation. It is a partnership with the parson as the captain of the ship. Ideally, both must aim to be on parallel wavelengths, taking an interest and concern in the work of the other. Each will inevitably have different points of view; there will be differences in personality which, through age, temperament and background, may sometimes be in conflict. Ultimately – and inescapably – it is a question of working together, a *modus vivendi,* but yet with independence. Surely this is not expecting too much?

It follows that consultation is the keyword. In no less degree good relationships with choir and congregation are necessary. In the final count, much of this joint ministry revolves around humility and the ability to deal with one's fellow creatures as human beings. Unfortunately, the failure frequency shows how often these basic necessities are ignored or brushed aside as of little consequence.

I therefore hope this book will be read, and in its entirety, by *all* concerned and that its objective, that of producing a fuller understanding of the respective roles of the parson and organist, will be realised.

In the average parochial situation, the parson has many commitments. The unmusical parson is therefore liable to write off music. But, the pastoral implications of music in worship, both in their own right and as they concern people, are immense and many sided. These I shall constantly underline.

Although this book may appeal more readily to the parson who cares about music and will consequently always find space for it, I hope it will also be read by the parson who is lukewarm, perhaps even by those hostile to the claims of music in worship. It may also have something to say to those who, on the face of it, 'couldn't care less'. The so-called 'musical' parson comes into a separate category; he can either be a blessing or a bane, often the latter.

The contemporary scene, with its new forms of worship and music, has resulted in considerable bewilderment and some-times even frustration. But, as I see it, what has really happened is equally challenging; it ought also to be stimu-lating and because it concerns people – robed or otherwise – will colour much of what I have to say.

Probably as never before in Anglican terms, there is a growing awareness of the value and necessity of corporate worship. Series 2 and 3, and now the ASB, have emphasised this. Even in some of our cathedrals it has permeated and sometimes wellnigh revolutionised Sundays, so I hope that what I have to say will also have some relevance to cathedral circles.

The special needs of the country parish, where the lot of the parson and his organist is frequently difficult and often disheartening, are as real in their way as the unbusinesslike attitudes which can so easily prevail in any church environ-ment. This is surely detrimental both for the image of the Church and for all concerned.

It matters greatly how worship is presented. An infinite capacity for dullness seems to permeate so much public worship and its music. Joy, enthusiasm and efficiency are three commodities hard to come by in some parishes, no less than is a sense of being visionary, versatile, and flexible in outlook.

Those who have read *Church Music at the Crossroads* will recognise certain hobby-horses which I feel need stating as much today as when I wrote my first book over ten years ago. For this I make no apology, nor for the frequent references to the facilities provided by the Royal School of Church Music, an organisation as unique in what it has to offer today as when it was founded over fifty years ago.

Above all, I hope this book will emphasise the need to do *all* things well, this the more so in a day and age where the attainment of excellence is so frequently suspect. Worship, if it is to realise its fullest potential, demands the best in every aspect, both visual and aural. It therefore demands effort.

Of the many people I have deliberately consulted while writing this book (not least those who, unsuspectingly and therefore without realising it, provided me with useful information), my especial thanks go to John Barrow, Sue Chapman, Cecil Clutton, Lindsay Colquhoun, John Cooke, Malcolm Cousins, Michael Fleming, Noreen Fortune, David Frost, Martin How, Robert McDowall, Richard Mulkern, Michael Nicholas, Michael Perry, Keith Rhodes, Michael Rhodes, Cyril Taylor, Vincent Waterhouse and Edred Wright.

For help and information from the Liturgical Commission, I am indebted to its former Chairman, The Very Revd Dr Ronald Jasper, and the Commission's former Secretary, Mrs B. Ebdale.

Finally, to my long-suffering wife who, as always, contributed much which others could not (and dare not), especially encouragement to complete the task.

If I have forgotten anyone it is because, in my quest for information, I picked so many brains on so many different occasions.

NOTE TO SECOND EDITION

On revising the text for this new edition, I realised just how much has happened in the past five or six years. I have therefore updated much of the information where this was needed and I have included reference to relevant new publications.

As the first edition was published in the days of Series 1, 2 and 3, I have deleted any such reference and have taken into account *The Alternative Service Book 1980.*

Among those who have been especially helpful in the preparation of this new edition, I would like to thank Canon Alan Dunstan, Donald Findlay, The Revd Norman Goldhawk, The Revd Alan Luff, Dr Bernard Massey and The Dean of York.

November 1981   L. D.

The Parson

Musical considerations as they affect him

THE PARSON AND THE CHOIR

Is music and a choir necessary?

The simple answer is that neither choir nor music are *necessary* to worship. Many services take place, and to good effect, without music. But most will agree that music can – and should – add a new dimension in making a service more complete and ideally more beautiful. Music impresses more readily than speech and is carefully provided for in the Book of Common Prayer. It does not matter how simple the music is. It is a matter of cutting one's cloth accordingly.

The plain truth is that good music, well performed and presented, helps to draw people into church. While music which is unworthy and badly performed turns people away from church.

A choir, properly instructed by parson and organist, will help to lead worship by participating in worship themselves. As a church organisation the choir should see themselves as part of the congregation singled out to do a specialised job, a role parallel to that of churchwardens, sidesmen or servers. A choir is certainly *not* an elite, dressed up for the occasion, placed on the stage four or five steps above the audience, separated from them by a screen and very likely entering and leaving the church by a different door. These are real dangers, often brought about by geographical conditions inherited from The Oxford Movement. Even so, merely to transfer a choir into the body of the church will not automatically solve every such situation.

Do you want a choir?

Do you see your choir as a necessary evil? Rather than encouraging and helping to build up their numbers, are you looking for the first opportunity of making depleted ranks or some other excuse an opportunity for disbanding them? Do you believe that the congregation will sing better on their own than with a choir (which they probably won't) or are you itching to 'be with it' and bring in a pop group? Are you afraid of upsetting your congregation, your choir, or both?

Search your conscience very carefully on this one; there is no automatic answer. Hasty action can result in more problems and disruptions than you bargain for. The age-old English compromise is probably the best long-term answer, if you are all going to live happily together as a Christian community.

Recruiting—how you can help

There was a time when recruiting referred almost exclusively to children, and probably boys at that. Today it means men and women as well, for relatively few choirs can boast of all the members they would wish to have. The incumbent should be in a position to know something of the potential field. No one would deny difficulties today in recruiting into any part of the Church's work. Attitudes of mind, attitudes of commitment towards the Church itself and the five-day week all help to deflect people away from church choirs.

The Church itself, for a variety of reasons, is sometimes partly to blame, not least when its services are dull and routine. It is equally true that when businesslike attitudes prevail and a choir is really worth joining, in all probability there will be no shortage of recruits.

Recruiting is one matter, but keeping members after the initial novelty has worn off is a different, and more time-consuming, proposition. There are obvious pastoral implications here. It is worth reflecting that Sir Sydney Nicholson, the founder of the RSCM, maintained that the boy chorister movement was one of the Church's best youth organisations.

Showing interest in the choir

No choir can be expected to exist solely on a weekly diet of hymns, Merbecke, and perhaps a psalm. All choirs must from time to time be allowed to shine in their own right, and be encouraged to do so by the parson. This stimulates them and is a means of gaining confidence and increasing interest in the job. Otherwise singers will eventually shift their allegiance to a church where the choir is given its reasonable head.

Be prepared to spend a few moments talking to the choir, and doing so with a genuine interest in them both as choir members and as human beings. Thank them for their contribution to the services and, above all, encourage them both to their faces and through the congregation and the parish magazine. All of us thrive on encouragement.

Involving suitable choir members of all ages to read lessons or the Epistle, and to do other tasks apart from ordinary choir duties, provide added incentives which will please them and help them to feel they belong more fully.

Some clergy ask if they should attend every choir rehearsal. This is neither necessary nor probably desirable, although the fact that you take the trouble to put in an appearance from time to time will tangibly show your interest.

Finally, do support your organist and choir, and not only by lip service. Consultation at all levels—and there are many possibilities in this respect—can do nothing but good. This is elementary psychology.

THE PARSON'S PERSONAL ROLE IN THE SERVICES

The said parts

The parsonic voice is as common today as ever. Though perhaps somewhat amusing when remembering it on a Monday morning, it is extremely frustrating if you are subjected to a weekly diet which mutilates beautiful language under the pretext of 'bringing out the meaning. . . .'

The inability to read and speak naturally is by no means confined to the older parson. Far too many clergy of all ages, having been well trained at their theological college, get into the habit of mumbling or, worse still, of rushing. A third fault, in an effort to be what is termed 'interesting', can render the message ludicrously overstated – 'Have mercy upon *YOU*'. How equally senseless it is – and insensitive – when the natural flow of language is ironed out into a dull monotony which ignores punctuation and spacing.

The pace of a service must be determined by the size of the building and the distance of the parson from the people. A common fault in reading prayers is that of slowing down at the end. Any momentum which has been established is thus destroyed and the result is an untidy or uncertain Amen from the people. Another infuriating habit is that of the parson who bellows out Amen before anyone has had a reasonable chance to utter.

'Hooly Ghoost' and 'AH . . . moon' are but two random examples of what not to do. I know both offenders and they speak quite naturally out of church and both have wives who obviously have not told their husbands.

Projecting the voice towards the far end of the church (this does not imply shouting), looking at the people, reading deliberately and with thought, using the *natural* rise and fall of words, timing, and putting it across in an interesting way, are fundamental principles too often ignored. The professionalism of the average television newscaster can offer much to those prepared to listen – and look.

Small points these, but they affect those on the receiving end and distract their thoughts from higher things.

Announcing hymns and anthems

'T is the Tone for giving out notices'.
(*Anglican Alphabet,* attributed to the Revd Sandys Wason. c. 1905.)

Announcements can, and should, be meaningful and compelling, but when muttered, shouted or overstated they have the opposite effect. I am sure the average parson is quite oblivious of the importance of clarity. As many churches have hymn boards and a weekly service leaflet, announcements need only be minimal. 'Shall we sing Hymn number 470?—(I always want to retort 'NO')—'The four hundred and seventieth hymn—Praise my soul, the King of heaven' merely assumes that the congregation have no intelligence.

This applies even more so when an unmusical parson sets about announcing an anthem. I recently heard, all in one breath, 'How beauteous are their feet who stand by Charles Villiers Stanford'.

The golden rule is 'Be sparing in the use of words and—be natural'. Why, when in church, adopt a deep and funereal voice such as you would never use at home?

Singing

Organists sometimes tend to judge their clergy solely on their singing ability. Although this obviously affects the musicians, it must be remembered that the average parson was not ordained primarily to sing his way to heaven on A flat.

Intoning, or the ability to sing phrases on a given note, especially when versicles are so often brief miniatures, is an extremely difficult task. It demands a high degree of perception, the ability to sing in the middle of the note (a common failing is to scoop up to the note), a relaxed yet controlled approach—and unending practice, especially when you think you are beginning to do it well.

The end product should sound natural, never dreary or routine and never too loud (this being the certain way of going out of tune). Pace and phrasing play the same role as in the spoken parts of the service.

In some churches it is now the custom for collects to be said, in which case the Amen ought also to be said. There is no justification for mixing the two. By custom it is only a bishop who has the right to sing the Blessing. If, for example, *Sursum Corda* is to be sung, it must be a really compelling invitation if the replies are to convey anything.

Your organist can help and encourage you to sing well by giving you a note which is neither too high nor too low for comfort. Both of you should be prepared to rehearse occasionally with the choir. Versicles and Responses are, after all, a combined exercise.

If you find it impossible to pitch a note with any semblance of accuracy, it is no real disgrace. Cut your losses and allow a suitable choir member to sing the versicles.

If your choir is small and ineffective, or perhaps non-existent, do resist a hearty bellowing, however well intentioned. In practice, it seldom encourages a congregation to give of their best; more often, the sheer volume of sound, accurate or otherwise, will annoy, exasperate, and finally silence them.

A parallel situation is the member of the congregation or choir—invariably a tenor—who sings inordinately loudly and by doing so imposes his or her whim on all within earshot.

Vestry prayers

Are these necessary? The Blessing, or Dismissal, at the end of ASB Rite A or B Holy Communion is final. If an extra prayer is tacked on at the end for the sole benefit of the choir, then let it be said in the vestry, preferably by one of the choir. A rousing organ voluntary immediately following the exhortation sending us 'out into the world' is far more positive than the nebulous walk to the vestry or West end, to the accompaniment of doodling on the organ, prior to yet another dismissal.

Punctuality and example

If you are unpunctual everything will be delayed. Jobs needing to be done before a service should be completed well in advance. From an expectant congregation's viewpoint nothing is less edifying than seeing the parson rush around making last minute preparations. A late start can soon become the accepted norm. Unpunctuality is an unprofessional lack of discipline.

Finally, much depends on the example of the parson. As the captain of the ship, his attitudes, his efficiency (whether or not he happens to be businesslike), will infect all, not least the choir and congregation. Detail—which is not triviality —includes how the parson walks, or waddles, when processing, how he sits, or slouches, and whether he stands errect or leans on the stall for comfort. As the choir and organist are usually placed around the parson, his influence in these matters is enormous.

FINDING, AND GETTING RID OF, AN ORGANIST

The first is as daunting a prospect as the second, for the demand far exceeds the supply. Nowadays relatively few people are prepared to be tied Sunday by Sunday, especially when an all too familiar pattern of uninterested, intolerant, or even hostile clergy, difficulties in maintaining a choir and the prospect of a pay packet which barely covers expenses, combine to put off even the most dedicated person.

Advertising a vacancy

The best avenues are:

Church Times (7 Portugal Street, Kingsway, London WC2A 2HP). Published on Fridays, this is a popular and well-proven hunting ground.

The Musical Times (1–3 Upper James Street, London W1R 4BP), needs copy six weeks in advance, as does *Musical Opinion* (The Bourne Press, 3–11 Spring Road, Bournemouth, Dorset, BH1 4QA). Both are published on the first of each month and are widely consulted by those looking for posts.

Local papers should never be underestimated; they often produce unexpected results. Some have a special system whereby an advertisment can appear simultaneously in a number of local papers in the same group.

It is useful to consult your cathedral organist or the organist of a major parish church in your area as either may be able to recommend pupils or know of someone suitable. Some Organists' Associations publish a list of members available to do duty at local churches. This also is worth pursuing although one of the most effective methods can be the word of mouth enquiry. It costs nothing and is often productive.

The wording of an advertisement needs to give enough information to whet the appetite; no more. Never waste money on details which can be discussed at a subsequent interview. Advertisements which include statements such as 'must be keen churchperson' or 'salary by arrangement' are best left unsaid, certainly in print. A sample might read something like: 'St. Hugh's, Hogsnorton. Organist and choirmaster wanted. Parish Communion and Evensong. Anglo-Catholic. Good 3-manual organ. Salary £ . . . p.a. Further information from . . .'.

References and qualifications

Never rely on a blanket type reference ('I have known Mr X for ten years . . . and can thoroughly recommend him for any post he may be applying for'). It seldom says anything of value, and it will probably be out of date and have been presented on previous occasions. It is better to ask for names of persons from whom a frank and honest opinion can be sought as to the applicant's suitability for a particular post.

If there are enough applications to warrant selection, do consult an experienced musician (your cathedral organist?) before drawing up a short list. Such action can be a helpful safeguard, if only to tell you whom to avoid.

Many first rate amateurs have no qualifications. This in no way reflects on their skill; far from it. But be on your guard for doubtful, valueless or even non-existent diplomas. If in any doubt consult your cathedral organist or the RSCM.

The interview

Have one or two key people from the church with you and give the candidates plenty of opportunity to put forward any ideas or suggestions they may have. Musical considerations are obviously important. Those interviewing should hear the candidate play the organ, and priority should be given on how he/she plays hymns rather than elaborate voluntaries. A church organist probably has to play more hymns than anything else and many who can perform their pieces brilliantly have no idea how to play hymns so as to bring a service to life and make people really want to sing.

It is equally necessary for you, the parson, to assess whether you feel you are basically on the same wavelength as the candidate and likely to be able to work together. If, for example, a candidate openly complains to you about his/her present vicar, he/she will probably be no less disloyal to you should an occasion arise.

The interview should allow both sides to feel free to express their opinions. What do you *want* of your organist? A 'yes' person? The candidate must by aware of pastoral implications and want to project these in his/her work. In this way he/she can do much to help you in your work. Is the person suitable for your particular parish and type of churchmanship?

Personality and all it implies should be as weighty a consideration as musicianship. While personality can conceal a limited musical ability, no amount of musicianship can cover up for a lack of personality.

These are but some of the considerations which should be taken into account. Carefully weigh up all the pros and cons and never appoint someone you are uncertain about simply because the choice is small. It is better to wait and be safe rather than sorry.

Finally, try to make an interview as informal as possible. Vicarage armchairs are more relaxing than a 'round the vestry table' approach. It will also help to put all concerned at their ease. In this way you can help the candidate to give of his best, especially if he/she is young and inexperienced at being interviewed.

Salary and contract

Everything should be clearly spelt out at the interview. The salary ought to take into account the present day value of money and the effects of inflation. The labourer should be seen to be worthy of his hire for you are more likely to get a good return for your money if you make a realistic offer. It is better to offer nothing than the near insult of something like £50 a year plus fees, with no thought for the travelling expenses of those living outside the parish.

Fees for weddings and funerals are an additional incentive both to an organist and the choir. People who use the church at such times merely for social convenience should be expected to pay in proportion to what they are likely to lavish on other aspects of the occasion. Members of the congregation should be expected to pay less than outsiders.

Duties and holidays need to be made quite clear and agreed by all concerned.

In the case of a professional musician, other work which might be linked with the post, such as school teaching, music teaching and musical activities in the neighbourhood, should also be discussed. Those interviewing should include some in a position to help in such matters. The added financial implications are an obvious attraction.

It should also be fully understood that the organist is allowed the free use of the organ for giving lessons, while pupils are charged a small fee for organ practice.

(See Appendix 1.)

However simple it is, a contract acts as a safeguard for both parties. It should clearly specify terms of service, duties, holidays, remuneration, method of terminating the agreement and, perhaps most necessary of all, retiring age. This last may be looking far into the future but can save possible embarrassment when the time comes. A verbal agreement is, on all counts, far from satisfactory.

The Royal College of Organists, Kensington Gore, London SW7 2QS, issues a carefully worded form of agreement. It is also obtainable from the RSCM and costs 15p. The agreement is, incidentally, between the Incumbent (employer) and Organist (employee), the PCC only being responsible for finding the employee's remuneration.

How to keep your organist

Do treat your organist as a colleague. It is a partnership with you as the captain, but you should be prepared to take an interest in each other's work. Otherwise it can never fully succeed. While each of you will obviously have different points of view, sometimes conflicting, in the final count it is the ability to live and work together in a parish community which really counts. Above all else this means that there must be consultation between you.

The final responsibility must of necessity be yours. While your organist must understand this, never use it as an unfair lever to exert pressure, however legal it may be. Don't adopt an aggressive approach from a position of strength.

Always encourage your organist to better himself, or herself, by consulting a reputable teacher or by occasionally attending one of the many refresher courses promoted by the RSCM. Some financial assistance from the PCC towards the cost will be an incentive.

An old dog of any age can be taught new tricks—if he/she wants to!

If you have a 'reluctant' organist virtually press-ganged into service because no one else was available, one of the regular four-day courses arranged by the RSCM at Addington Palace can be invaluable. Staffed by those who understand the particular needs, these courses give basic help on how to approach playing the organ as a pianist—and they are always enjoyable occasions.

How to get rid of an organist

This is often much more difficult than keeping one. The devil you know, complete with faults, is possibly preferable to the alternative of no organist and little prospect of finding one. This is not helped if a disgruntled organist spreads the word around that you are a difficult person to work with. Are you?

The wise parson will carefully weigh up the pros and cons before taking action. Hasty and ill-considered moves can easily result in your having a choir revolt on your hands. The essence is tact and you may well have to swallow some of your pride in the process. The last state could be much worse than the first.

Even so, it is worth bearing in mind that as most clergy and congregations consider music to be a desirable part of worship, the present shortage of organists leaves the market very much on the musician's side.

THE PARSON CHOIRTRAINER

As with the 'reluctant' organist, persuaded to play for services because no one else is available, or willing, to do the job, the chances are that you may assume the role of choir-trainer for similar reasons.

Here, then, are some hints on how you might advantageously proceed:

1 Be yourself, and be aware of your own shortcomings. At the same time be patient over the shortcomings of your choir, who are also human beings.

2 Inspire and encourage your singers. By doing so you will help to make them *want* to sing. They will soon sense whether or not you have the ability to draw the best out of them.

3 Keep the choir well occupied by giving them plenty of variety in their work.

4 Consult them from time to time. Merely because you happen to be the vicar does not mean that you present them with what you currently believe to be right, irrespective of what their view point might be.

5 Gain as much help as you can by reading books on the subject (including this one). Whenever possible, observe other choirtrainers in action and make full use of the services of the RSCM.

6 Use common sense and tact at *all* times, especially when things are not going well or you are feeling liverish.

7 Remember that nine-tenths of choir training, especially on these terms, is persuading people to sing naturally—and with real enjoyment—while aiming for the best possible result. This, incidentally, can frequently be a really high standard—if you are prepared to take the necessary time and trouble.

8 The more experience you gain, and the more you are prepared to be constructively self critical, the more likely you are to become a good choirtrainer. On the other hand, the rot will soon start to set in once you start to be satisfied with your efforts.

WITHOUT ORGANIST OR CHOIR

In circumstances where there is no reasonable expectation of finding an organist and where there is no choir and so few parishioners that everything would otherwise have to be said, long playing records and cassettes are now available.

The Church of Ireland has issued 143 records of hymns, psalms, canticles and voluntaries. All are of the 7-inch, 45 r.p.m. type. Full details can be obtained from the Secretary of the Recorded Church Music Committee, Church of Ireland House, Church Avenue, Rathmines, Dublin 6, Eire.

WHEN IN DIFFICULTY . . .

The RSCM, with the accumulated experience of many years, is in a unique position to help. This it does in two main ways:

1 *Affiliation,* the benefits of which are set out in Appendix 2, automatically puts members in touch with the facilities offered. In the light of this it is strange that a number of those who are members, and faithfully pay their annual subscription, do little or nothing about getting some return for their money.

2 *Courses,* either at Addington Palace or at local level. Addington Palace, a fine eighteenth-century house set in spacious parkland only twelve miles from central London, is now an ecumenical education centre for *all* concerned with the Church and its music. With an annual programme of around 60 courses, ranging from one-day events to residential courses of up to six weeks, some are promoted specifically for the clergy. These include:

> The Church and its music today—and tomorrow?
> Liturgical teach-ins
> Refresher courses on the conduct of services
> The parson and his organist
> Religion and music in school chapels.

The Addington courses are promoted on a national level but those 'in the field' are at present administered on a diocesan basis with local needs being specially catered for. Addington will always be glad to provide information on what the dioceses are doing.

The current brochure for the courses at Addington can be obtained from the Warden. Study it carefully. It contains a wealth of information on events for organists, choirtrainers and choir members, and is designed to be helpful in the widest context. While fees are kept as low as possible, the cost of travel may prove a barrier to some. On a number of occasions PCCs and others interested in helping the music of their churches have subsidised persons wishing to attend courses. This gesture encourages and is appreciated by those concerned.

Most RSCM courses are specially directed towards needs at the *average* parish level, which is by far the largest area of the church music scene.

On a diocesan level, do consult your cathedral organist. Nowadays, the majority are extremely approachable and often have a wider knowledge of the local situation than they are sometimes given credit for. Many really do want to help, an encouraging contrast to the ivory tower attitude of the less enlightened nineteenth-century scene.

If you are feeling stale, one of the RSCM refresher courses could prove a stimulus. The active discussion which takes place has been found invaluable to those taking part. Today there is no need for any parson to be isolated.

At any rate, when stale, frustrated, or longing to make a new impact, never resort to gimmicks. A full house is not significant if the people go just for sensation, or for something controversial and maybe 'with it'. These are factors which can easily blind people to what worship—and the Church—is all about.

It is equally doubtful whether shock tactics impress the congregation any more than the choir. The first time the vicar stands on his head in the pulpit it causes something of a stir. Having done it for three successive weeks it becomes a tradition.

Always remember that *you* can either help or undermine your organist's work and he/she, to a degree, yours. By your example, especially in such matters as reverence, the general conduct of services and behaviour in the vestry, you can do much to help, or mar, musical matters. Again and again in these pages I revert back to personal relationships.

2

The Organist and/or Choirtrainer

In most cases, the organist is also the choirtrainer. While this is not always the most satisfactory state of affairs it is one dictated by force of circumstances. What follows is therefore directed at the one, or the other—or both—and necessarily consists of generalisations.

SOME TECHNICALITIES OF ORGAN PLAYING FOR SERVICES

Four general and basic pointers are worth bearing in mind:

1 Keys, both on manuals and pedals, must be depressed and released together. This tidiness is a fundamental discipline. Failure to do it will be especially noticeable at the beginning and end of anything and will reflect adversely on the choir's performance.

2 The ability to accompany in the most effective way as opposed to leading. This is the more relevant where there is no choir. It demands unerringly rhythmic playing, at the same time transmitting that extra something which will encourage people to want to sing. A compelling rhythmic vitality will have more effect than merely pulling

out every stop and turgidly dragging the congregation
along. Sheer volume of sound acts as a depressive to those
on the receiving end.

3 Your personality inevitably emerges through your fingers
and feet, for you possess the power to make or mar the
music of the services. The organist can inspire the choir and
congregation to efforts beyond their normal selves.

4 Because an organ often sounds different in the body of a
church than when heard at the console, it is helpful to listen
to someone else playing so that you can judge for yourself
the effect of the organ as heard by the congregation. This
can sometimes be an unexpectedly revealing experience.

The accompaniment of the services

Apart from training the choir, this is by far the most important part of the organist's work. The playing of pieces,
although important and necessary in its own right, must be
seen as a secondary role.

How to play hymns

In the course of his/her work the average organist probably
plays more hymns than anything else, and in doing so involves
himself/herself with others. It is therefore the more unfortunate that this aspect of his/her work is so often regarded as
of small importance. Because it is thought to be easy—which
it isn't—it is seldom given its due priority.

Almost for the first time in my life I am now a member of a
congregation and therefore on the receiving end. By and large
I have found it an unedifying experience, often frustrating
and traumatic. Dull, unrhythmic and unimaginative playing,
often inaccurate, clumsy, and with little relation to the
sentiment of the words, are some of the negative qualities I
experience.

It seems to me, as far as hymn playing is concerned, that

few organists possess either the ability or, worse still, the desire to relay anything, least of all inspiration, to either choir or congregation. In a word, hymn playing is frequently viewed as a chore.

Here then are some conclusions, as I see them:

1 Most hymns seem to be played at a more or less uniform speed, whereas the mood of words and tune should determine tempo and style, and therefore interpretation. Ideally, no two successive hymns should move at the same speed.

2 Hymns must be played accurately and not 'improved'— accidentally or intentionally—by the addition of extra notes or other elaborations. They must also be played loud enough to be readily audible by the congregation in the body of the church.

3 Insecurity, and often instability, results from playing over a hymn at one speed (with a sizeable *rallentando* at the end) followed by an entirely different speed when the singing commences. Similarly, a *rallentando* at the end of each verse destroys any rhythmic impetus previously established.

4 For most purposes, one or even two lines is quite sufficient for the 'play over'. Anything longer will usually detract from the momentum which is one of the objects of an introduction. (The congregation should be encouraged to stand immediately the play-over begins.)

5 When the introduction ends on the dominant chord, it is inartistic and thoroughly confusing to add an extra chord or two in order to arrive back at the tonic. Similarly, employing the last two lines of a tune as introduction is, for similar reasons, equally indefensible.

6 Gaps between verses must be consistent and rhythmic, not determined by the time needed to change fistfuls of

stops, nor so short that those singing have no chance to breathe.

7 How necessary it is to follow the words and to phrase accordingly. Do you merely play the requisite number of verses, with the last verse automatically louder than the rest?

8 Word punctuation can be the more effectively mirrored in the playing by lifting the right hand while the left hand and pedals maintain a *legato*. Notice, by contrast, the far less effective lifting of *both* hands and pedals.

9 The sense of the words determines the choice of stops. Much of the uneventful registration I hear would seem to negate this.

10 The variety of stop permutations available, even on the smallest organ, is much greater than is often realised. (See Appendix 3.)

11 Many tunes, especially in *Hymns Ancient and Modern,* are pitched too high for vocal comfort in the melodic line. As an organist I did not accept this; as a member of the congregation I know it to be true! If you find it difficult to transpose at sight (as many people do), either write out the tune in the new key or get a copy of the Transposed Edition of *Hymns Ancient and Modern.* This is much more ethical than trusting to luck—at the expense of your unsuspecting congregation.

12 Always be conscious of rhythm. It equates vitality with interest, ingredients not always found in the performance of church music, as many hymns do not automatically seem unduly rhythmic. As a help, think of as few beats as possible—two in a bar instead of four, and one in a bar in triple time. The dangerous habit of prolonging the length of the last note in each line is further evidence of unrhythmic playing. Greater rhythmic perception is needed in

quiet or slow-moving hymns than in the more boisterous or loud ones.

Some further points, especially when there is no choir:

1 Play the pedals at the correct pitch. It is so easy to get into the habit of playing in the bottom octave of the pedalboard.

2 Make the sounds as reassuring as possible:
   (a) Not only change combinations of stops, but use stops individually.
   (b) Avoid the incessant use of Open Diapason tone. Reserve it for climaxes while concentrating more on *light* 8-foot sounds, with 4-foot stops added for brightness.
   (c) Remember that congregations are more aware of sounds above (i.e. 4-foot and 2-foot pitch) than sounds below (pedals).
   (d) A slavish adherence to *Ancient and Modern* expression marks can often produce ludicrous results.

Finally, the playing of hymns and, for that matter, of psalms, must be lively and helpful to both congregation and choir, and in that order.

The accompaniments of some modern hymns, such as those by Sydney Carter and Geoffrey Beaumont, are far removed from the traditional style. Many are pianistic in conception and have a distinctive left hand chordal structure which demands the use of the sustaining pedal. It is a style of writing which fails to come off effectively when played note for note on the organ. Such hymns can only sound convincing if carefully rearranged in terms of the organ.

Descants. These come into two categories, those to be sung and, less frequently, those to be played.

If you have enough sopranos or trebles a descant can be

akin to the icing on the cake. It can also be an inspiring climax to a hymn or in certain verses in the psalms. A descant must be thought of as a counter melody moving in partnership with the original tune which, being sung by tenors and basses in unison, provides a tonal contrast. Neither is more important than the other.

A descant is not an opportunity for a choir to show off by singing as loudly as possible on high notes, nor need a descant be necessarily confined to the last verse. For example verses 3 and 5 of *All people that on earth do dwell* both qualify for descant treatment as do verses 3 and 6 of *Bright the vision that delighted*.

Good descants are not always easy to find. In addition to certain standard hymn books such as *A and M Revised* and *Congregational Praise,* there are good examples in some of the recently issued supplements.

Alan Gray's *A Book of Descants* (Cambridge) is variable in content but has been out of print for some years.

Some of the best are those tailor-made for special occasions, e.g. Christopher Gower's for *Ye watchers and ye holy ones* and Sir William Harris's version for the final verse of *Now thank we all our God,* both of which can be found in RSCM Festival Service Books.

Descants for the organ are what is usually referred to as 'playing over the top', that is, transposing a mixture of the alto and tenor lines so that they become a new melodic line. This is a variant which can add much to the artistic effect if well prepared and executed. If done off the cuff it can easily throw everyone out, not least the organist, so never be ashamed to write down such variants.

These, incidentally, are the type of melodic outline which help to make the psalms in a cathedral sound so beautiful. As such, they are made up on the spur of the moment and no two versions are alike. But you need to be very experienced to do this sort of thing well.

Using part of a chant by Robert Cooke, a typical example might be:

In the absence of a choir, there is much to be said for playing a hymn descant on the organ, similar to the above chant.

Free accompaniments. A free accompaniment also needs a careful approach. Don't embark on it unless you can improve on the original. If at all uncertain, write it out. Never trust to luck—or inspiration; both are likely to let you down at the crucial moment.

A free accompaniment should add to, and heighten, the total effect; it must never detract from the business in hand or, at worst, embarrass.

The RSCM publish a collection of 50 *Accompaniments for Unison Hymn Singing* while a long out-of-print book of *Varied Harmonies for Organ Accompaniment,* issued by the Proprietors of Hymns Ancient and Modern, reveals a wide and at times extravagant range. Some are hopelessly over-loaded with notes and lush harmonic context—these are a frequent failing in many such attempts—but Charles Macpherson's two versions for *Bright the vision* are surely some of the most exciting ever written.

Transposing hymns. Although most choirs have a rooted objection to hymns being transposed down (and it must be conceded that it sometimes takes altos, tenors and basses excessively low), it must be remembered that hymns are one of the occasions when a congregation can really sing, the more so when it is a big and special event. Many tunes, especially in A and M Revised (AMR) are too high for congregational comfort. *St Albinus* (EH 134) and *St Helen* (AMR 400) are both melodically uncomfortable in C major but a different proposition when transposed down a tone (as the former is in AMR).

There is seldom a need to transpose up, except where the key of F major is concerned. Being in this dull key, tunes such as *Albano* (AMR 398) and *Kocher* (AMR 289) both gain by being played in F sharp major.

(See Appendix 4.)

Responses

Mattins and Evensong. Most churches use the so-called Ferial version. It matters not whether the responses are sung in harmony or in unison, with or without accompaniment. More to the point is that they are sung lightly and in speech rhythm, as you would say them in normal and unhurried group conversation. Some Victorian versions, such as *The Cathedral Prayer Book,* where almost every word or syllable is forced into a musical time value, still linger on here and there. As they contradict all the laws of natural speech, no amount of rehearsal can ever make them sound convincing.

The Creed, as a corporate affirmation of faith, is nowadays almost universally said, as also frequently are the Lesser

Litany and Lord's Prayer. In the spoken parts of a service, the appallingly dreary mumbling which many congregations and choirs affect is indefensible. It is unreal in terms of normal life and normal conversation; its almost automatic use in church only reinforces the view held by many that churchgoing is a dull and unrealistic occupation.

For special occasions, settings by Tudor or twentieth-century composers are sometimes sung by a choir. They can be alternatives provided the congregation accept that they are for the choir, and the choir alone. The same applies to responses at weddings, where a simple version for choir can heighten the sense of occasion.

Holy Communion. For Sursum Corda, whether or not pre-faced by 'The Lord be with you', etc. the customary plain-song is best sung unaccompanied and in unison. All these responses must be sung lightly if they are to have musical integrity.

In all instances the priest's part is of great importance. Every parson should therefore expect (and be expected) to rehearse with the choir from time to time. The choir's singing will for the greater part be made or marred by the parson's singing. For those clergy who really cannot sing and find it both a worry and an embarrassment, there is no reason why the versicles should not be sung by a suitable member of the choir.

ASB responses are dealt with in Chapter 4.

Psalms and types of psalter

A wide variety of psalters is in existence. As each sets out to promote a particular theory on how the psalms should be sung, it is probably helpful to mention the merits or other-wise of some of these.

The Cathedral Psalter and *New Cathedral Psalter* were the first in the field. In trying to make the words fit the chant instead of the chant being the musical vehicle for conveying the words, it is hardly surprising that many extremely awkward moments exist, especially in short verses of the canticles. The misrepresentation is heightened by the use of heavy type for a number of unimportant words and syllables.

The Oxford Psalter, edited by Henry Ley, Stanley Roper and Hylton Stewart, appeared in 1929, and *The Worcester Psalter* in 1948. While both are workable examples of how best to approach speech rhythm, the look of the printed page is formidable and, in the case of *The Oxford Psalter,* makes it difficult to follow, the more so when some verses abandon the colon and become 'run-through' verses.

The Parish Psalter, the work of Sir Sydney Nicholson, is by far the best for most practical purposes. Its pointing is simple, consistent, and easy to read, while its popularity at all levels, not least among the congregations Nicholson had in mind, is proof of its suitability.

All these versions use the traditional Coverdale translation in the Book of Common Prayer.

More recent developments have led to varying types of approach. *The Revised Psalter* (1966) is the work of a distinguished body of theologians, poets and musicians entrusted by the Archbishop of Canterbury with the task of removing 'obscurities and serious errors of translation, yet such as to retain, as far as possible, the general character in style and rhythm of Coverdale's version and its suitability for congregational use'. Despite its pointing being akin to *The Parish Psalter* it has never caught on and is used in only a handful of churches.

The Revd Christopher Wansey has produced an interesting *New Testament Psalter* which contains 7 canticles and 55 psalms paraphrased in the traditional form of psalmody.

Father Laurence Bevenot's *15 Psalms to honour the Holy Eucharist* have a certain affinity with Gelineau but are simpler and more direct.

The Liturgical Psalter would seem to be far and away the best modern translation yet *in terms of singing.* As each psalm was newly translated, it was carefully scrutinised to ensure that the text was in fact singable. This is the psalter included with *The Alternative Service Book 1980*.

Collins Liturgical Publications have subsequently published an edition which, together with the ASB Canticles, includes Anglican chants, the choice of music having been made on similar, and sometimes identical, lines to those in *The Parish Psalter*.

The psalms as treated by Joseph Gelineau, a Belgian Jesuit priest, have an interesting approach. Capable of being performed in a number of ways, each according to available resources, the characteristic refrain, or antiphon, can soon be learned by a congregation. Fifty-four of the Gelineau psalms, each with its distinctive quasi-plainsong style, are published in two books by The Grail (England).

Psalm Praise is another recent attempt at a new-style approach to the subject. In realising that 'The psalms are among the richest parts of our Christian heritage', *Psalm Praise* approaches the psalter in a variety of ways, some of them quite novel. Metrical versions, side by side with traditional psalmody pointed for use with Anglican chants, are interspersed with others treated in a free contemporary vein. Because of the many composers and styles employed, much of the music is understandably variable in quality, some of it regrettably trivial.

These, then, are but some of the ways in which the psalms can be musically treated. In looking to the future and to fresh experimentation it must be said that if satisfactory ways of singing the psalms cannot be devised, there is a risk that we shall lose touch with them. In the final count, whether it be the worst examples from *The Cathedral Psalter* or the latest in speech rhythm, everything hinges on *how* the psalms are sung. I have heard admirable sounds from the former and deplorable results from the latter.

For the actual playing of the psalms, here are a few helpful hints:

1 Know your chant from memory so that you can concentrate fully on the words.

2 Sing the words to yourself as you play.

3 Think in phrases and look ahead.

4 As with hymns, the mood of the words should determine
   the dynamics, the 'colour' and, perhaps most important of
   all, the pace at which a psalm should be sung.

5 Phrasing. This is as essential for the organist as for the
   singers. All punctuation and the ends of verses must therefore be clearly marked.

6 Be sparing in the use of pedals and reserve them for verses
   of special emphasis.

7 Always remember that the *Gloria* is the culmination of a
   psalm. It must suggest this and never sound routine,
   repetitive, or an afterthought. The same applies to the
   canticles, the singing of which can so easily become uneventful through familiarity.

8 Differing schools of thought exist as to how a chant should
   be 'played over'. Although arbitrary, the semibreve/minim
   notation does provide a desirable element of shape
   otherwise absent when the chant is played in a timeless
   way.

Chants, and chant books

Although in theory the available choice is wide, in practice
this usually narrows down to the frequent use of a few
examples. Be adventurous and do not confine one particular
chant to a specific psalm or canticle. There are many good
chants of all periods, the only reservations being:

1 For general parish church use avoid chants with high
   reciting notes, and

2 Be sparing in the use of passing notes. While some help to
   preserve the individuality of the music, others merely

thicken the texture and make it the more difficult to achieve speech rhythm. While each chant must be judged on its own merits in this respect, it is generally wisest, if in doubt, to discard passing notes rather than keep them.

The custom which dictates that *Venite*, *Jubilate* and *Nunc Dimittis* are sung to single chants seems pointless. As so many single chants are dull, there is much to be said for dispensing with this practice, especially for *Venite* and *Jubilate* which call for an exciting musical treatment.

Certain psalms need a change of chant where the mood of the text alters. Verse 8 of Psalm 6 and verse 14 of Psalm 51 are examples of this. The new chant should be in a related key with choir and organist taking care to produce a unanimous join. The custom whereby the organist loudly plunges into the new chant in advance of choir and congregation as if to say 'I'm ready and will show you I am' is thoroughly inartistic— and helps no one.

While some psalters, such as *Old Cathedral*, *New Cathedral* and *Parish* have chants for each psalm, a number of separate chant collections are available, the best known being *The Anglican Chant Book* and *The RSCM Chant Book*. Some well known examples are common to most collections.

Many cathedrals have their own home-made collections. These often contain some interesting examples not to be found elsewhere. Most cathedral organists will, within reason, allow their use outside the cathedral but will appreciate a stamped addressed envelope when you write to seek permission.

Plainsong (Contributed by Michael Fleming)

Plainsong has never been widely used in the worship of the Church since the Reformation, but it must be remembered that no part of our musical heritage has a longer history while remaining fundamentally unaltered. Plainsong has a validity unbounded by time and is as relevant to the liturgical needs of the Church today as it was 1500 years ago.

There are those who say that Latin is the only correct language for plainsong, but much of the music of the early church was sung in Greek and, of course, the Oxford Movement brought the need for an English translation in the nineteenth century, so there is no reason why plainsong should not be adapted to modern English texts.

As churchmanship has become a word of rather less importance these days, so also should plainsong cease to be thought of as the musical representative of the Anglo-Catholic wing of the Church. It is encouraging to see an increasing need for this kind of music, and not only in the Anglican communion, for it has much to commend it. The popularity of the Office of Compline, with its regular broadcasts, shows that here is a way in which plainsong can be introduced into contemporary church worship.

The psalms are much easier to sing to plainchant than to any other form of music. Being in unison, this method of psalm singing is ideally suited to small congregations or churches where there is no choir. The hymns are often more difficult but there are quite a number of simple Office hymns and most congregations are able to cope with the *Veni, Creator*.

Although no accompaniment was originally intended, a background of harmony on the organ does help to mellow the austere nature of the chant, provided it always remains unobtrusive. Its real function, however, is to keep the singers in tune.

One of the singular qualities of plainsong is its unique character. Apart from folksong, there is nothing like it anywhere else in musical or religious experience, and it is in this very detachment from secular associations that its strength lies. It is true liturgical music, having grown up in hand with our liturgy from the earliest times and it is indeed 'the perfect marriage of melody, words and worship'.

Four useful books:

Dom Anselm Hughes: *Plainsong for English choirs* (Faith Press).

J. H. Arnold: *The approach to Plainsong through the Office Hymn* (Oxford).

Dom Anselm Hughes: *Practical Plainsong* (Burns and Oates)

Walter S. Vale: *Plainsong—an outline of its theory and interpretation* (Faith Press).

Mary Berry: *Plainchant for Everyone* (RSCM).

Anthems and service music (see pages 77–81)

Any comments here can only be generalisations. Choirs range from balanced and proficient SATB groups to an ill-assorted collection of people, probably doing their best (if they have been properly taught) but whose ability is restricted. In all instances circumstances must dictate the choice of music. The degree of difficulty must be within the capabilities of the singers, never overwhelming them simply because the choirtrainer wants to try out the 8-part Palestrina motet he recently heard in King's College, Cambridge.

Never underestimate good simple music. It is much better to sing simple music well than difficult music in an indifferent and probably unconvincing way. Think of the listeners.

Every choir, however humble, should try to build up its library in a systematic way. The purchase of music and its introduction can often be determined by planning the musical year in line with the needs of the Church's year.

For depleted choirs, there are a number of unison and two-part anthems, of which *The Oxford Easy Anthem Book* and various RSCM publications are useful examples. Alternatively, it may be necessary to arrange existing music for a smaller choir, in which case it is advisable to seek the help of someone qualified to deal with the task.

Never shun the use of appropriate hymns and psalms as

anthems; it is a useful way of introducing less familiar examples of both to a congregation. The RSCM's *Sixteen Hymns of Today for use as simple anthems* is, in this respect, a particularly useful collection.

There are occasions when the choice of music should be stimulating and challenging; given suitable conditions, it will help increase the efficiency and confidence of a choir. For churches with adequate musical resources there is much to be said for the growing tendency to perform suitable continental music, such as the Masses and motets of Haydn, Mozart, Schubert and twentieth-century French composers. These can be valuable in a context where liturgical traditions allow their use. In the final count it must always be a case of cutting one's cloth accordingly, bearing in mind that anthems help to offset the routine which can so easily result from the repetitive nature of our services.

In all instances the importance of unaccompanied music cannot be over-estimated. The aural and general training it demands is of immense value to any choir.

Even if recent liturgical moves have tended towards emphasising the role of the congregation, there is a place for anthems and motets which even the most unmusical clergy could scarcely fail to deny. The Series 3 *Seasonal Sentences,* published by the RSCM, are an example of how such miniatures can be integrated, and to good effect.

Nowadays it is difficult to know with any accuracy what choir music is available, what is out of print and what is deleted. With the demise of so many provincial music shops, browsing through catalogues or reading advertisements is of little help in itself. This is especially so where recent, and therefore unknown, publications are concerned.

At the RSCM we sometimes ask one of the publishing houses to arrange a sales promotion exercise as part of a course. Complimentary copies are distributed and recordings played. This is a useful way of coming to terms with publishers' recent issues; it also helps in assessing what is viable to any given situation.

Some indication of current trends can be seen from the fact that many publishers now find it more economic, both for themselves and their customers, to issue collections of music instead of single copies.

Copyright

The need for complying with the regulations governing copyright cannot be over-emphasised. A comprehensive booklet entitled *Copying Music,* gives full information on all aspects of the subject; this includes helpful advice on when music may be legitimately reproduced. Copies of this booklet may be obtained, free of charge, from The Music Publishers Association, 7th floor, Kingsway House, 103 Kingsway, London WC2B 6QX.

As ignorance of the regulations governing the Copyright Act is no excuse for irresponsible photo-copying, all church musicians and clergy are urged to get a copy and through this to be in full possession of the facts.

Voluntaries

The choice here being so extensive, a few general guidelines and suggestions must suffice.

Never in any way play down the immense editorial work of C. H. Trevor, whose capacity for discovery was limitless, as for example, his six volumes of *Old English Organ Music for Manuals,* published by OUP. Even by 1981 standards £8.40 is a very fair price to pay for 85 pieces, each with editorial and biographical notes.

Nor is two-stave organ music confined to the seventeenth and eighteenth centuries, as witness some interesting examples by both English and continental composers of the last century and today. Although there are organists who have, on principle, an inverted superiority complex about playing music without pedals, the more discerning know better.

Whatever the proficiency of the player or the resources of

the instrument, what does matter is that voluntaries are chosen with care, bearing in mind their suitability to any given occasion. The right choice of music can influence a service as much as can bible readings, collects and hymns.

Choose voluntaries well in advance (*not* during the sermon), and practise them. There is nothing clever in an 'on the spur of the moment' choice which can lead to dire sounds being inflicted on the listeners.

Five minutes of carefully chosen music before a service can create the right atmosphere in no uncertain way, especially if there is no competition with the bells, which always seem to be in a key entirely unrelated to any organ piece.

The concluding voluntary need not always be loud, nor need the opening music always be soft. Variety and aptness must always be taken into account. For example, triumphant music at Christmas or Easter can be a thrilling sound, the more so when it leads directly into the introit hymn at the Eucharist. A short 'middle voluntary' at the Offertory, during the Administration or even sometimes in place of a Gradual, is proving a popular new departure, especially in the Anglican church. (See Appendix 5.)

Improvising

There are two main places in a service where short extemporary interludes may be called for:

1 If the Offertory hymn is too short (which it ought not to be if chosen with proper care).

2 Between the blessing and a final voluntary while the choir recess before a vestry prayer.

Unless you are a born improviser it is extremely difficult to do it convincingly and artistically. It is so easy to meander and so difficult to produce a miniature. Yet many organists try to improvise with little thought or adequate preparation.

As pointers, bear in mind that time, key and phrase must be constantly in evidence as basic necessities. While economy of texture is an over-riding consideration, it is far harder to improvise in three- or two-part writing than in a four-part hymn tune style. The final result should sound inevitable and musical, not uneventful and routine. Although improvising can to a certain extent be taught (it is taken very seriously on the continent) those who are best at it have an instinctive flair for what, after all, is a specialised art.

ON LEARNING THE ORGAN

A *good* teacher is essential, and therefore exhaustive and careful enquiries are essential. Neither the local parish church organist nor your cathedral organist may, for many good reasons, be the right person for your particular needs.

If you fail to find the help you want, you can go a lot of the way on a do-it-yourself basis. Tutors such as C. H. Trevor's *The Oxford Organ Method* or Buck's *The First Year at the Organ* (Stainer and Bell) can be worked through on one's own and implemented by regular lessons, say once a month, on a consultation basis. Although personal lessons are the obvious ideal, they may not always be practicable. Evening classes, where they exist, can also be extremely helpful, especially when the tuition is really on a class basis with the members observing and learning from each other.

How to practise

What is important is not the amount of time spent at the console but *how* the time is occupied. It is possible to play for two hours non-stop and yet to have learned little in the process. Shorter sessions packed with systematic hard work are likely to be far more productive.

Whenever you make a mistake deal with it immediately. Isolate it, see why you went wrong (it will often be only a small fundamental error such as fingering) and put it right there and then. Never gloss over errors, however well-intentioned you may be over coming to terms with them next time round. Similarly, when learning pieces, do not always necessarily commence every practice session at bar one. Sometimes start in the middle and concentrate on the latter half, or make a mental note of the difficult passages and work exclusively on these.

In the end, what matters is seeing and hearing the results of your labours. By dealing once and for all with difficult passages you then approach them with confidence instead of dread. In this way your entire approach is disciplined and your playing will benefit enormously.

Nor should these principles be applied solely to pieces. If anything, hymns, anthems and service settings need even greater emphasis when practising, for here playing involves others who are dependent on you. Your security, or lack of it, will also be theirs.

This ultimately leads to the experience of playing in public, a very different proposition from that of playing to yourself in an empty church.

Enlarging your horizon

Do not confine your interests to organ and church music. If you include the experience of other types of music you will, if you are perceptive, benefit your work for the church.

Orchestral music can reveal much about texture, colour and style, as will listening to chamber music. A study of the string quartets of Haydn and Mozart will show much in common with the linear texture Bach used in his organ Trio Sonatas. The romanticism of Brahms, Mahler or Richard Strauss, in terms of the orchestra or opera, will help in understanding the architecture and colour of much nineteenth-century organ music.

The world of organ and church music is not an isolated pursuit having no relation to the musical world at large.

Courses and qualifications

The RSCM promote a constant supply of short courses ranging from weekends for teen-age organists to refreshers for older people. As most of the courses are graded according to ability or experience, the aim is to cater for all needs. Although primarily at Addington Palace, some are promoted on a national basis. An Adult Training Scheme has also been started, details of which can be obtained from Addington.

For the organist who wants to gain further experience and wishes to work towards specific goals in terms of examinations, there are a number of possibilities:

1 The practical examinations in organ playing as conducted by the Associated Board of the Royal Schools of Music. The syllabus covers a wide range of expertise, including sight reading and aural tests, with transposition in the later grades.

2 Practical organ examinations are also part of the work of Trinity College of Music and the Guildhall School of Music.

These examinations are conducted at local level in centres and churches throughout the country. In most instances it is possible for organ candidates to be examined on the organ of their choice.

For the more advanced, and in order of difficulty, there are:

1 The examinations of the Incorporated Guild of Church Musicians leading to the Archbishop of Canterbury's Certificate in Church Music. These examinations can now be taken in most parts of the world.

2 The diplomas of the Royal College of Organists. The Associateship (ARCO) must be passed before proceeding to the Fellowship (FRCO). The Choirmasters Diploma (Chm), which includes a thirty-minute practical examination with a choir, is restricted to holders of ARCO and FRCO.

3 The Archbishop's Diploma in Church Music, administered
   jointly by the RCO and the RSCM, is restricted to those
   already holding both FRCO and Chm. An exhaustive
   knowledge of liturgy and specialised periods and subjects
   (such as Hymnody and Plainsong) is required.

4 The Royal College of Music and the Royal Academy of
   Music both conduct organ examinations at diploma level
   (ARCM and LRAM). Candidates can enter either as
   teachers or performers, the latter being required to give a
   recital at a high standard of performance. The playing
   requirements for the teacher's diploma are less exacting,
   but the examination includes a viva voce devoted to a
   knowledge of the organ and how to teach it. These examinations also take place in most of the Commonwealth
   countries and are conducted by visiting examiners from the
   U.K. The requirements for overseas are practically identical
   with those of this country but with only one diploma,
   Licentiate of the Royal Schools of Music (LRSM).

   (Appendix 11 gives the addresses of the examining bodies
mentioned above.)

THE RELUCTANT ORGANIST

With the present day demand for organists far exceeding
the supply, churchgoers are unexpectedly finding themselves
transferred from the pew to the console. Are you such a
person, and were you recruited because all efforts to find
someone else had failed and the Vicar knew you once played
the piano? If so, the chances are that you will not only feel
inadequate but have certain reservations – and with good
reason.

Some of the best supported Addington courses are those
which aim at converting pianists into organists, especially
those who are 'reluctant'. They are tailor-made to help those
who know little about playing the organ or training the choir,
who are probably daunted both by the prospect of having to
do so and perform in public.

It is encouraging to see how quickly confidence can be gained, the more so when the reluctant performer finds it quite within his grasp to play the organ without having continually to use those forbidding pedals.

At local level, a number of LEA evening classes together with the more visionary Organists' Associations, now cater for the needs of this important and relatively new aspect of church work.

THE WORK OF THE CHOIRTRAINER

Some general points, whether or not he/she is also the organist.

Choir training in its widest sense

Far too many books have been written on the subject and I have no intention of adding to the complexities of what should be a relatively straightforward matter, given some common sense, both in teaching methods and in dealing with those on the receiving end.

The best vocal sounds are those which are produced naturally and with ease. The worst usually come from those whose voices have been 'trained', often by someone concerned with theories and methods alone.

Boys usually sing with such ease because they seldom think about technique. By contrast, the adult is often preoccupied with the voice as such and can sometimes be so worried about it that technical problems, real or imagined, over-ride artistic considerations.

It is reported that Varley Roberts, the blunt Yorkshireman at one time organist of Magdalen College, Oxford, said that it was merely a question of opening the mouth and singing – a dictum with more than a grain of truth in it. That surely is what singing is basically concerned with, and in these ways:

1 Natural and pure vowel sounds.

2 Natural clarity of consonants – no more and no less – to help give the singing coherence, vitality and rhythm.

3 A relaxed and enjoyable approach, and

4 Probably most important of all, the ability to listen both to one's self and one's neighbours, the necessity for which seems to escape the singer in a way it never would a string player, who is equally responsible for making his own notes.

But all of these factors will be of no avail unless the choir-trainer knows how to teach. He/she must instinctively be able to hear what is wrong, tell the choir, and put it right. Only by doing so will he/she be able to instil a sense of standard and achievement.

Conducting

Be sparing in your gestures. You are not conducting the Royal Choral Society in the Albert Hall. Any such extravagance distracts a congregation even if it satisfies your ego and makes you feel you are a budding Barbirolli or a Previn.

As many church choirs are unaccustomed to being conducted, your hands and facial expression should communicate what you want of them, having first trained them to look at you, and understand your indications. Then they can react accordingly.

The more you conduct from memory and the more your choir learn to sing without burying their heads – and their hearts – in their copies, the better you and they will be able to concentrate on interpretation which, after all, is what music should be concerned with.

Economy of gesture is always an asset, especially when conducting in church. By beating a relaxed two-in-a-bar instead of a jerky four, and one rather than three, you will visually encourage your choir to produce a more flowing and legato phrase shape. A vigorous waving of the arms produces exactly the opposite effect and should be reserved for those occasions when the music demands it.

Many choir conductors use the same type of gesture whatever the music may be, and then wonder why their choir sings everything in the same way.

Tape recording as an instructional aid

This can be invaluable; it can also be a salutary experience for all concerned. While it is one thing to be told by a third party how good or bad your performance was last Sunday, it is another thing to hear for yourself the sounds you actually made. The wise person will draw his own, if private, conclusions and be the better for it.

Used sparingly, and never as a substitute for teaching, the tape recorder can be of great help and encouragement provided all concerned realise that recording can sometimes make a choir sound better than it actually is.

LP records can help to give ideas as to how works can be performed and what they sound like, but frequent hearing tends to make the performers adopt that particular interpretation at the expense of their own.

Relationships with church organisations

Make it your business to be on good terms with your PCC, Finance Committee, and other parochial bodies. Nothing but good usually comes out of relationships created without ulterior motives. Then, when ulterior motives do arise you have made links and helpful friendships.

As mentioned earlier, too frequently and through no fault of their own, the positioning of a choir and organist in the chancel tends to cut them off from the congregation, making them into a separatist body, often without their being aware of it.

You and your choir are as much part of the parochial scene as the congregation should be part of yours.

GENERAL

Are you stale, or out of touch?

Being a church organist can be a very lonely occupation. Because of the necessarily repetitive nature of the services and because an organist works on his/her own, tied to the church for perhaps fifty Sundays of the year, it is easy to become stale and out of touch with changes and developments – and usually without realising it.

New thought and stimulus is essential for us all. The old dog, the older he becomes, can – and must – learn new tricks. Concerts, recitals and festivals (not necessarily of church music) are but some of the ways of keeping the mind open and receptive to new ideas. Discussion with other musicians is another way of avoiding that rut of inbred conservatism which can so easily infiltrate into the Church.

Today, with endless opportunities for hearing music on the radio, television, and through recordings and concerts, there is much less excuse for being cut off than a generation ago. Any such isolation is therefore a self-imposed one.

The advantages of taking every such opportunity are obvious. They help the organist to tackle the task recharged with new ideas for himself/herself, the choir and the congregation. The experience will help when times, methods and personal attitudes are changing. The following organisations and periodicals should prove useful:

1 *The Incorporated Association of Organists.* A national body consisting mainly of local organists' associations. Its annual Congress, held in a different centre each summer, draws about 300 people from this country and overseas, and includes in its programme a wide variety of lectures, recitals and visits to organs. The IAO's quarterly journal, *The Organists' Review,* contains interesting articles and news items. The Secretary of the IAO is Roger Bishton, Hampton House, Leigh Road, Bradford Leigh, Bradford-on-Avon, Wilts. BA15 2RW.

2 Most Diocesan Choral Associations promote an annual festival for church choirs. It is usually held in the cathedral and is conducted by the cathedral organist and is an ideal opportunity for choirs to meet each other and to sing together in their mother church. It can also be a stimulus, especially for small and remote country churches whose choirs return home with renewed vigour and incentive.

3 Musical periodicals:

(a) *The Musical Times* has a section devoted to the RCO and to general organ and church music news.

(b) *Musical Opinion* is rather less scholarly and devotes considerable space to articles, organ news and correspondence.

(c) *Church Music Quarterly,* the house magazine of the RSCM, is sent free to all affiliated choirs and Friends of the RSCM. It contains articles, news items, reviews, photographs, a section for choristers, and a variety of advertisements.

(d) *Church Times,* published weekly on Fridays, is a useful all-purposes church newspaper on a national scale. It keeps readers informed of current ecclesiastical news and some of its articles are provocative. From time to time church music items are included.

(e) Membership of the Royal College of Organists brings with it the annual handbook containing a full list of members and their posts, presidential addresses and other relevant information.

The addresses of 3(a) and 3(d) are to be found on pages 7 and 8, and that of the RCO on page 11.

How to go about looking for a job

This was spelt out in terms of the parson on pages 7-12. Much the same is applicable to the organist. There is one subtle distinction: the need to consider the churchmanship of a parish in relation to yours. If you are low church you will probably be unhappy in an Anglo-Catholic environment and *vice versa*. Organists sometimes gloss this over as unimportant, but subsequently find how real it is.

Consider all angles. If you are first and foremost a choir trainer, look for a church which will give you scope in this direction. Similarly, if you are more of an organist, bear in mind the opportunities of a church with a good organ.

References. The wise applicant will no more hawk around a blanket reference, which is probably out of date, than will a discerning parson accept such a document. It is far better, and much more to the point, to ask your referee to write specifically about your suitability to the particular post in question. But do ask first. It is both impolite and presumptuous to name a referee without having first asked his approval. For my own part, anyone who quotes me for a reference without having asked my permission goes down in my estimation and usually gets a less unqualified recommendation than might otherwise have been the case.

At your interview, be certain to ask *all* the questions you want to. You have as much right to be fully informed as have your prospective employers. Having been appointed, make certain you have a contract, and one which spells out everything quite clearly – salary and fees (to be periodically reviewed in line with inflation), duties, holidays, the right to use the organ for teaching pupils, and your own right of practice on the instrument.

It is worth the expense of asking a solicitor to give it approval so that there are no loopholes, accidental or otherwise. Then, and only then, sign it.

SUMMING UP FOR THE CHOIRTRAINER—AND ORGANIST

1 Do you know your own capacity and capabilities?

2 Do you know the true nature of the beast which is yourself?

3 Are you argumentative, inflexible, and a 'doing the Almighty a favour' type? Is this rubbing off on your choir?

4 Are you broadminded, attuned to those around you, and able to lead them to better things?

5 Are you a practising and believing Christian? Do you therefore accompany the services sympathetically and with an understanding for liturgy and worship?

6 Do you constantly encourage and help your choir? Are you constructive, not destructive, in your criticism?

Be you the organist, the choirtrainer, or both, always be ready to learn by experience and, not least, by privately – but honestly – assessing yourself.

3

The Parson and the Organist

Quite apart from the personal considerations and needs of both parties – dealt with in Chapter 1 (The Parson) and Chapter 2 (The Organist and/or Choirtrainer) – we now deal with certain aspects which jointly affect both parties.

For example, while hymns and their tunes should be the responsibility of both parson and organist, anthems must be the prerogative of the organist, though it is always wise to discuss forward planning with the parson.

If good personal relationships were looked upon as essential to any partnership, far fewer problems would arise, not least in matters concerning the Church and its music. To tolerate and respect the other point of view and to be prepared to act on it, is difficult for many clergy and organists. The fact that music is ultimately the legal responsibility of the parson has been known to result in a misplaced power complex, especially if the incumbent is unsure of his ground. The same can be said for the so-called musical parson. A man with a little knowledge can easily get under the skin of the organist who may have rather more knowledge, while such an attitude can soon undermine his/her authority with the choir.

But, on the other hand, the organist concerned with music only and not with worship, can equally prove an embarrassment to the vicar.

In many of the subjects discussed in this section, the advice of a cathedral organist can, and probably should, be sought to advantage – providing he/she is an approachable person and understands the parish point of view.

THE ORGAN

General care and maintenance

An organ must be kept in good repair and regularly tuned, in much the same way as the wise car owner ensures that his/her vehicle is regularly serviced. It is equally important that a reputable firm be employed, preferably the builder of the instrument.

A contract should be entered into, bearing in mind that the cheapest tender may not necessarily produce the most reliable work.

As a generalisation, most organs need tuning at least twice a year. Circumstances, such as dampness or variable temperatures, may necessitate three or four annual tunings. This is more likely in a church which, unheated for six days in the week, is probably subjected to the dry and probably excessive heat of a coke boiler on Sundays. Much also depends on the size of the organ, the condition of the reeds, its general age and its reliability.

Many nineteenth-century organs, solidly built by real craftsmen, need surprisingly little maintenance, just as some small modern organs with mechanical action need a minimum of tuning and regulation. It is impossible to suggest any general yardstick; each organ must be judged on its own merits and record.

A notebook should be kept on the console and any mechanical faults noted as they occur. This is helpful to the tuner if he is to give the best service.

Cleaning and overhaul

The average organ will need such attention every ten to fifteen years. Whether it gets it is another matter. Most churches accumulate more dust than is generally apparent and this, after a period of time, inevitably affects the delicate mechanism of an organ, noticeably the action.

Servicing and oiling of the blower at regular intervals by a reliable electrician is also essential.

How to go about rebuilding

A number of factors need to be carefully considered before coming to any final decision:

1 What in fact *needs* doing? This is not necessarily what the organist wants. The organist may dream of the prestige of a large organ with every conceivable accessory, but the parish which is expected to pay for it looks at it differently. Some organs are extravagantly large for the church, while others can be too small to support the singing.

In recent years the techniques of voicing have been revolutionised. Individual stops can now have more clarity, direction of sound, variety and character. Organ design and mechanism have likewise undergone considerable technological changes, and all for the better.

Modern tracker (mechanical) action, if made by a firm who really knows its job, is very different from the heavy and uneven touch of many an existing nineteenth-century instrument where the action is probably long overdue for renovation. In terms of reliability there is little that can go wrong with good tracker action.

2 Where should the organ be situated? If the existing instrument is in a boxed-in position in the chancel, it will almost automatically be taken for granted that it must be moved into the body of the church. This is not always the right answer, nor is the need for a detached console, another status symbol of many an organist.

A mobile organ should not be ruled out, especially in modern multi-purpose churches where the furniture is constantly being moved.

These are matters to be carefully taken into consideration. They depend on architectural and acoustic factors on which expert advice should be sought.

3 The cheapest tender is not always the best. Cutting costs in order to secure a contract is a known practice in most walks of life. In the end you only get what you are prepared to pay for – no more and no less. There are no short cuts, for good and enduring work is inevitably expensive, and organ building is a craft. Despite mounting present day costs, it is a false economy to go for something on the cheap.

It is equally unsatisfactory to draw up an ambitious specification much of which can only be completed at some future date when funds allow. It is much better to plan according to a reasonable expectation of funds, and build a complete instrument.

It is wise forward planning to set up a fund for organ maintenance and depreciation, for which the PCC might earmark a certain sum each year.

For most congregations, a rebuilt organ will sound little different from what it did before, except that it may be louder. If you are appealing for funds, it is a good psychological move to clean the organ case and front pipes. This gives people a sense of seeing something for their money.

4 Which builder? To suggest the pros and cons of specific builders is to beg the question and would probably prove libellous. Suffice it to say that some builders are more suitable than others in a given situation. For example, while certain small firms have a reputation for concentrating on first-rate small organs, they would not be suitable for, nor probably willing to undertake, a large rebuild.

The pipe organ versus *the electronic instrument*

This is a vexed subject, highlighted by the extensive publicity given to electronics which, on the face of it, offer highly attractive features.

A leaflet, *Electronic Organs,* issued jointly by the Royal
College of Organists, The Incorporated Association of
Organists, the RSCM, the Organ Advisory Group (Roman
Catholic) and the Organs Advisory Committee of the Council
for the Care of Churches,carefully outlines the pros and cons.
Copies can be obtained from any of the five sponsoring
organisations, whose addresses can be found in Appendix 11.

On seeking advice

As most restoration work will require the approval of the
Diocesan Advisory Committee and a faculty (or legal permission) from the Diocesan Chancellor, it is wise to consult the
Diocesan Organs Adviser in the first instance. His expert
knowledge and experience can be of immense help. The golden
rule, if in doubt, is to seek advice from the Diocesan Registrar
on whether a faculty is needed or merely, as in the case of
cleaning (without any alterations), an Archdeacon's
certificate. Permission of one sort or the other is required for
all work carried out in Anglican churches.

It is unwise to go ahead without official Diocesan approval.
Such action may lead to a consistory court at which, as the
ultimate sanction, the Chancellor can order that the organ be
returned to its previous state (for example, if unauthorised
additions have been made).

The Organs Advisory Committee receives limited funds
annually from charitable bodies such as the Pilgrim Trust for
allocation towards the careful restoration of organs with
casework or pipework of historic interest. Application should
be made to the Clerk to the Organs Advisory Committee,
Council for the Care of Churches, 83 London Wall, London
EC2M 5NA.

**THE USE OF INSTRUMENTS OTHER THAN THE
ORGAN**

Why always the organ? As the traditional musical instrument
in church it is thought of as being 'sacred'. But there are a

number of possible and probably desirable alternatives, whether for the sake of variety or because a parish is suffering from the current scarcity of organists. It is generally easier to find a pianist than an organist.

Considering the vast sums of money earmarked by successive governments for education, including school music, it is sad to reflect how little of the resulting expertise filters back into the church and its music. The remarkably high standard achieved by school children in string, wind and brass ensembles could surely be sometimes employed to advantage in the church. A little thought and imagination could soon produce some excitingly colourful additions to the singing of hymns and other music.

Cultivating such links with schools can also help in recruiting boys and girls to join church choirs. It can also have pastoral implications through involving otherwise uncommitted parents and bringing them into church.

The piano

There are a number of very good reasons why a piano might be used in church. Its percussive quality can often encourage congregational singing more readily than the organ. Its mobility means it can be placed near to the congregation, even in among them, while the combined use of organ and piano can produce an inspiring sound.

The harmonium

Take every precaution to avoid its use. It is virtually impossible to play the instrument rhythmically and, because of its large and snarling noise, the melodic line can never be properly heard. Whichever stop is drawn makes little or no difference, and it looks so ugly.

THE ORGANIST

Although the work of the organist as such has been dealt with at some length in other parts of this book, there are certain considerations which jointly concern the parson and the organist.

A periodic refresher course should be viewed by the organist and choirtrainer as a matter of course. The fact that it so seldom is invariably reflects apathy, contentment with things as they are, or a built-in and probably stubborn resistance towards anything which may show up deficiencies or demand some effort towards a new look.

This demonstrates a lamentable attitude which can ultimately only have a bad influence on choir and congregation.

An organist can take advantage of evening classes or attend the residential and one-day courses provided by the RSCM either at Addington or elsewhere. Most of these courses emphasise service work rather than the playing of pieces, for which help can be sought in other ways. Nor should lessons with a reputable teacher be ruled out, especially consultation lessons on a refresher basis.

A grateful PCC will encourage their organist to give his/her work a new look by paying, or at least helping towards paying, the necessary fee. Despite the increasing demands on parochial finances, this is money well spent to improve the services. Many PCCs do help in this way, and their support might perhaps be extended towards the incumbent, who might also benefit from fresh thought on the conduct of services, choice of suitable music and his relationship with the musicians.

DEPUTY ORGANISTS

Every encouragement ought to be given, especially to young people, to take up playing the organ and gain practical experience by becoming a deputy. The opportunity of playing in public is an essential part of the training of any musician. Most of those who have risen to an exalted station in musical life began in a humble way as an assistant, helped on their way by their local parson.

If a young parishioner shows a willingness to play for

services, the PCC could well make organ lessons possible. This will not only aid his/her personal progress, but may mean that the youngster eventually becomes a regular organist and be able to serve the Church in this capacity. Now that organists are scarce, this could be most valuable.

Students who already help by accompanying anthems and playing for occasional services might be further encouraged by being allowed free practice.

The use of the organ for practice by outsiders

Pupils of the organist and others may wish to use the organ for practice. This is reasonable enough and it is difficult to understand why some incumbents so adamantly refuse to allow it. Providing the privilege is not abused in any way, is kept within reasonable hours and the electricity paid for – the amount being agreed between the Parish Treasurer and the Organist – there seems no reason why permission should not be given.

THE CHOIR

How to recruit—and keep—a choir

This has always been a hard task, but is more difficult today when so many are frequently unwilling to accept any regular commitment and when the young are often openly encouraged by parents to come and go as they wish. The choirtrainer must continually think up ways of retaining the interests of the singers, whatever their age.

While the parson and the local schoolteacher should be obvious recruiting agents, the best (or worst) recommendations will come from those already in the choir. If a choir is progressive, efficient and businesslike, and therefore worth joining, the word will soon get around and such a choir will seldom, if ever, be short of potential new members.

Unwise is the choirtrainer who, on principle, resents girls

in choirs. Adult women can be another, and perhaps more formidable proposition, the more so the older they become. Problems surrounding adolescents can be equally tricky. Nevertheless, in certain situations it is girls and women or no top line at all.

In this, as in other respects, the efforts of many first-rate choirtrainers have been impaired by their inability to deal with their singers as human beings, in or out of choir. A sad, but true, fact.

Keith Rhodes is a person who has made a special study of recruiting, especially when he was organist of Bradford Cathedral. He relies on approaching schools with a properly organised plan of campaign, believing that choirtrainers are often too modest about what they can offer children. Many parents will encourage their children to join anything they feel will do the children good, if they are convinced that it is worthwhile. It costs very little to have a child in a church choir but, if the choir is efficient, it is likely to give a good, character-building training which will help in later life. This has been proved again and again, not least in the long tradition of our cathedral choirs.

Mr Rhodes has produced an informative and well presented recruiting leaflet which is worth studying. His address is 16 Briarwood Grove, Wibsey, Bradford, BD6 1SF.

Building up the choir

A church choir needs to be well organised. Most children actually value discipline (which really means orderliness), and parents will admire and appreciate something which is business-like and achieving a good standard of performance. But there are hazards to be coped with. Uninterested parents who exert little or no discipline and are more concerned with a weekend of leisure than with any commitment to the Church, town parishes depleted because people are moving into the suburbs, today's many distractions, not least television, the diminishing role of loyalty; all combine to form a malaise which eats like a cancer into every walk of life. To combat these, the parson and the organist must join forces to make membership of a choir so worthwhile that it eclipses favourite television programmes. Everything must be interesting, vital, and convincing – three attributes not always to the fore in church circles. Similarly, there must be 'out of choir' interests.

Woe to the parson who opts out of choir responsibility. His pastoral opportunities in dealing with choir members cannot be underestimated.

Attending to details

The way in which a choir processes in and out of church, the way it stands, sits and kneels, will inevitably be reflected in the efficiency of the singing. Make no mistake about this. Simple, yet dignified uniformity of movement, not to be confused with regimentation, is necessary, the more so when a choir sits where it can be seen by the whole congregation.

The same applies to the clarity and neatness of the said parts in a service. Tidy choir stalls and an organ console uncluttered by debris ranging from dirty handkerchiefs to toffee papers provide a reliable pointer as to whether the choir and organist are efficient.

Processions as such seem to be declining in popularity but if they are embarked upon, all concerned, whether clergy, servers or choir, must ensure that every movement has been carefully rehearsed. It is most impressive to watch a procession in those cathedrals and churches where careful preparation has been made. The opposite is an appalling spectacle. In this context, I might mention Alan Dunstan's admirable little book *These are the Hymns* (SPCK), which could be read advantageously. His views on singing a hymn merely to cover up movement from point A to point B are worth thinking about.

All these considerations apply most forcibly to the parson, whose example ought to be impeccable. Regrettably, some clergy seem to delight in being what is nowadays termed

casual, being under the impression that informality helps
people to feel more at ease in church. Perhaps this is a way of
evading responsibility for something which constantly needs
to be kept up to the mark.

It is often in small ways that general efficiency seems to fall
down. All concerned need to have a constant awareness of
the importance of their work and the need for care, reverence
and humility.

Where to sit and what to wear

As the East end of most churches is being increasingly aban-
doned in favour of a free-standing altar in the nave, so choirs
are tending to move out of the chancel into the body of the
church. Choirs can now be found in various places, one of
the most popular and sensible being behind the altar and
facing the people.

A choir visible to the congregation means that their every
movement, legitimate or otherwise, is seen by all. They must
therefore realise that any movement, fidgeting or talking, can
be a distraction to the congregation. Pillars and low arches,
especially those in medieval churches, can easily obscure the
visibility of choir and congregation.

Should the choir be robed? This is not vital though, on
balance, probably desirable. A well turned out choir can be a
visual aid to worship in much the same way as are vestments.
Costs will be the main deciding factor.

It should be borne in mind that choir robes need not be the
traditional cassock and surplice. The unisex monk-like habit
now gaining in popularity, is simple, dignified and highly
practicable, as are other new types of choir robe. As many of
these innovations are attractive and do not require constant
laundering or cleaning, there would seem to be much to
commend in their use.

Cash discounts on choir robing and choir accessories are
available to RSCM members from J. Wippell and Co. Ltd,
who are the official robe makers to the RSCM. Their head

office is P.O. Box 1, Cathedral Yard, Exeter, EX4 3DW. They also have branches in London and Manchester, with a United States office at 1300 Plaza Road, (P.O. Box 456), Fairlawn, New Jersey 07410.

Should the choir communicate?

As part of the corporate family witness of the parish, it is highly desirable that the choir communicate at a weekly Parish Communion. Ideally, they should go up to the altar before the congregation so that they can be back in their places for any music involving them during the communion of the people. Those not yet confirmed sometimes go to the communion rails and receive a blessing from the priest. They are easily identified as unconfirmed if they cross their arms when at the altar rail.

Staying for the sermon

It is questionable whether children should be subjected to two sermons each Sunday. While there is much to be said for their going out before the sermon at Evensong, the Parish Communion is a different proposition, the more so if the sermon is reasonably short and interestingly devoted to real teaching.

Some organists and clergy provide books on a variety of subject matter for the young to read during the sermon. Is it not more to the point to train the young to concentrate on listening for a few minutes?

Refreshments and transport

It is kind, and humane, to provide refreshments for a choir, especially when members may have travelled quite far, perhaps early in the morning or late on a weekday evening. As the social life of many parishes hinges to an extent on after service coffee or excuses for tea parties and the like, why not the choir?

To transport the choir is a much appreciated gesture, especially when people live some distance from the church. The best plan is for a certain person, or persons, to be responsible in rota for choir-members living in a given area. This volunteer taxi service may be arranged by the Vicar, the organist, or by members of the congregation. For the latter this is a further practical way of showing interest in the choir.

Parents' Associations

The more I see these in action, the more convinced I am of their value. In a number of ways they provide a working liaison between the choir and the church; they can support choir activities with a vested interest through catering or helping with the transport mentioned above. They can help parents to meet on a social level and can also support the raising of church funds.

Bearing in mind that a choir generally concerns only one or two members of a family, a Parents' Association is a useful means of involving the rest of the family. It seems strange that so few churches have such an organisation, though an increasing number have a choir club. It could surely be a further vehicle for pastoral work.

Families in choirs

This admirable pursuit seems to be growing and should be encouraged. It provides a ready-made opportunity for a family to do something useful as a unit, to do it for the Church, and to enjoy themselves in the process. It can be a source of great encouragement to organists short of choir members, especially when a family holds its own private choir practices at home.

Should the choir be paid?

Differing factors determine each circumstance. For boys and girls, despite the knowledge that they can earn so much more in other spare-time activities such as newspaper rounds and baby sitting, choir pay still remains an incentive with pay day eagerly looked forward to. Weddings and other extras all help to swell the pay packet.

There is much to be said for a sliding scale, worked out in line with experience and seniority, while a bonus for especially good work and general helpfulness will never come amiss.

In the average parish church the adult members are seldom paid, except sometimes for weddings and funerals. The reasons for this are obvious. Your church, as with many other similar organisations, is probably looking for ways to cut back on expenditure, therefore whatever you pay is likely to be unrealistic in modern monetary value, but you are at least showing willing by offering a token.

Some of the many London churches come into a different category. With virtually non-existent resources within the parish, the alternative to a paid choir usually means no choir at all. The considerable musical traditions of a number of City and West End churches are thus catered for by students from the London colleges of music who often form small, though highly efficient, professional-style choirs.

Incentives

No choir can exist solely on a weekly diet of hymns and psalms, with Merbecke perhaps thrown in for good measure. Recitals, musical services and other lollipops provide extra incentives, accentuating the work of the choir and helping to give it confidence and encouragement. Out-of-choir social activity is another way of knitting together the members into a happy and contented group the more likely to sing as a unit.

There are many side issues which help to create an efficient choir. A rehearsal packed out from start to finish with interest, variety, and the right type of choirtrainer enthusiasm, so that the choir goes home confident that they really know next Sunday's music, is but a further example of the efficiency which will repay handsome dividends and help to retain interest.

The basis of teaching should instil a constant awareness for standards, so that the members of the choir themselves want to become more proficient and versatile. By the reverse token, the choir whose singing meanders along in an aimless way, devoid of care for detail not only when singing but in the said parts and deportment, will soon project its malaise to those on the receiving end. For better or worse, everything a choir does, both aurally and visibly, feeds back into the worship of the church.

The wise choirtrainer will be visionary, especially over such routine matters as hymns, psalms and responses. He/she will be venturesome in the choice of chants and will avoid constantly linking one particular example with a specific psalm or canticle.

Responses and Amens need an equally searching review from time to time to avoid their becoming lethargic and routine. Everything, down to the smallest detail of what is said or sung, should *at all times* be of the highest possible standard. In other words, the familiar ought ideally to become a new experience on each successive hearing.

All this needs concentration and a sense of purpose. The choirtrainer will be demanding a lot of the singers and of himself/herself, but the chances are that they will respond more quickly to this type of treatment than a lukewarm approach, lacking in vitality or drive. And, in terms of the young, this all contributes towards training for life.

Everything ultimately depends on the choirtrainer, who must see that he/she knows the job down to the smallest detail. Because the choirtrainer is a human being dealing with other human beings, he/she will constantly feel frustrated and depressed, but should *never* show it. The challenge of the task should be its greatest stimulus.

Musical incentives. Recitals highlight the particular work of a choir and are therefore desirable occasions for them to shine on their own. A short recital might occasionally take the place of the sermon, though it will more usually be a separate event on a weekday evening. As there will be inevitable expenses such as printing and advertising, it is advisable to have a priced programme. By a strange quirk of human nature, most people value something they pay for more than something they get cheaply or for nothing.

Choral festivals, either on a local or diocesan level, are another incentive. Choirs relish the experience of being part of the big sound, they enjoy joining forces with other choirs and singing in a different church, especially their cathedral, and with a different conductor from whom they are likely to pick up a number of new points and food for thought. They may even hear familiar comments and criticisms reiterated by another voice.

Most cathedrals are on the lookout nowadays for good visiting choirs when their own choir are on holiday. This can be a further stimulus and thrill to any self-respecting parish choir but it is advisable to apply well in advance as most cathedrals now have many such requests.

Competitive festivals are a way of gaining constructive criticism from an experienced musician, while by singing to a secular audience a choir can make itself known to a wider public.

The RSCM Chorister Training Scheme is an added stimulus. Details of this worthwhile venture can be had from Martin How at Addington.

Joining forces for a Sunday evening service with choirs from other parishes, including Free Churches, is a valuable way of getting to know and understand other denominations. This has added meaning when the respective congregations can also be persuaded to merge.

Social incentives. The wide range of out-of-choir activities is also stimulating. Into this category come obvious recreational pursuits, not least the choir camp for those so inclined. This is

the more valid when linked with Sunday services in a church
near the camp.

Choir funds

As most of us, even today, value more something we have
ourselves had to work and pay for, there is much to be said
for setting up a choir fund. This can then be used to help
provide new music, outings and other pursuits, without
having to ask the Parish Treasurer on each occasion.

A choir can be proud of having raised money to provide
their music. Having paid for it themselves often means that
they value it the more—and the chances are they will look
after it the better.

How to cope with difficult choir members

Choir members who resist any suggestion of retirement, their
voices and possibly their mental faculties being impaired,
need to be handled with extreme tact. Although they may be
a liability to the choir, their age and probably their long
service in the choir will attract a measure of sympathy from
many in the congregation who will judge the issue more from
an ethical than a musical viewpoint.

Every choir at some time possesses a difficult person, and
no two instances are likely to be identical. It can only be
stressed that great tact (a quality not always to the fore in
church circles) is at all times called for. The leopard,
especially when ageing, is not likely to want to change his
spots. If he knows he is cornered he will probably become
more stubborn and difficult.

As with an elderly organist reluctant to give up the reins,
this may well be a cross one has to bear. Here is an opportunity to apply Christian charity and humility.

Conclusions

1 The choir must be aware of its responsibilities both towards the congregation and church worship. Intelligent

interpretation of the music stimulates and enriches the worship of the congregation.

2 The choir wields considerable power as an instrument of evangelism. This may not always be apparent to every member, though the wise choirtrainer will constantly impress this on them.

3 Regular attendance at rehearsals and services is of major *personal* importance. Anyone whose membership is on a casual basis is a liability to the efficiency of the choir as a whole.

4 Mutual consultation (and this includes consultation between the organist and the choir on the choice of music) may have good results. A contented choir is more willing to give of its best. Two heads are better than one, however qualified the one thinks he/she is.

5 Think carefully and with an open mind on mixed choirs. In the end, circumstances will usually dictate policy, unless those in charge confuse principles with reality.

6 Pay constant attention to detail, such as said parts, deportment and the singing of routine responses and Amens. These are *not* trivia.

7 Both parson and organist need constantly to encourage their choir. We all thrive on encouragement because we are human, not least in church circles.

GOOD AND BAD IN CHURCH MUSIC

'One man's meat is another man's poison.'

Much church music obviously depends on personal taste, preference and association. Most of us know what we like, which means we like what we know, even if it is bad. To be content with the familiar can often be equated with a fear of change, and the 'change and decay' of Lyte's hymn is sometimes cynically interpreted as change meaning decay.

Part of the problem lies in the bewildering amount of music from which to choose, together with its variable quality. There has been something of a revolution in hymnody in the past twenty years. The net result has been a two-stream development with a broadening growth of the traditional, vividly offset by the counter claims of the 'popular' element.

Into the first category come a number of new collections often in the handy form of supplements. Many are ecumenical in content and contain words and music which are positive and relate to the Church and the world today. Of these, *100 Hymns for Today* and its successor, *More Hymns for Today,* are probably the best known and most widely used. Fred Kaan, Erik Routley, Pratt Green, Cyril Taylor, John Bowers and Brian Wren are a representative cross section of those most active in this context.

'Pop' church music appears in great profusion and is surrounded by a special type of glamour which woos the unsuspecting. Its appeal to the younger age groups is understandable for it speaks a musical language familiar to them in everyday life. It may also prove to be just as ephemeral. Whether this new look is a suitable vehicle within the context of Christian worship is another matter and one which cannot be lightly dismissed.

A glance, for example, at the work of the Twentieth-century Church Light Music Group—whose hymns are so popular in schools—reveals a degree of mediocrity and poverty of musical invention which would be hard to equal anywhere, even in the worst excesses of many Victorian hymns. It is unwarranted to say that these hymns are liked by the young, who are often far more discerning than we give them credit for.

Many see the current vogue for groups and choruses as an unedifying distraction in the context of worship. They view it as something alien and a threat in itself to the establishment— both of which it probably is.

Any 'way out' move will 'attract admirers and devotees for

a time because there are always people to be found who delight in something new, whether it possesses enduring qualities or not—a matter which only time can show'.*

Contemporary church music ranges from the superficial and tawdry to much that is superbly good and relevant. This second category includes the use of folk songs, of which *Waly Waly* and the music of Sydney Carter are but two random examples. To keep track of all that is available is complicated enough; to differentiate its quality is even more demanding. To assume that *all* Victorian church music is bad is as misleading as to assert that *all* twentieth-century 'pop' is good or suitable for use in church. There is a very real danger in the angry young (or not so young) curate who is convinced that he, and he alone, knows what is wanted, and who envisages that the only way to salvation is through *young* people jiving their way to heaven on a glorious free-for-all bandwagon. The hard line inflexibility frequently engendered by such an attitude of mind makes it even more dangerous.

We must bear in mind that the many changes we are witnessing are far too near us in time to be assessed with reliability. Popularity does not necessarily imply that something is good. Various factors determine why that which works in one situation and one parish is quite out of place in another. Good music can be made to sound as dull as 'pop'—and *vice versa.*

Is the music ultimately the parson's responsibility?

What was said earlier can only be underlined, namely that the wise parson will work in partnership with his organist concerning the choice of hymns and psalms, and also in matters of general policy. He will delegate what they mutually agree upon. A rational appraisal by both parties ought to produce a *modus vivendi* without much trouble.

---

*John Ireland—a short study, by Cyril Scott (John Baker)

How much music?

What should be the extent of the musical content of a service, apart from hymns and psalms? There can be no hard and fast blueprint here as the needs of any given situation, not least the choir's ability, will largely determine what must ultimately be a finely balanced compromise between the interests of the choir and those of the congregation.

In some parishes there is now a weekday Evensong once or twice a month in which the choir are given their musical head. This is an admirable custom which deserves to be expanded. Even within the context of the ordinary Sunday services there should from time to time be a place for settings of canticles or special versions of the responses. Any reasonable parson and congregation will welcome this, provided it is kept within bounds and generally reserved for special occasions.

HYMNS

How to use the existing book to advantage

As hymns probably provide the greatest musical continuity in church it follows that the contents of any book should be used as fully and intelligently as possible. No one book will ever completely satisfy everyone. It must be reiterated, loud and strong, that hymns should be chosen jointly by the parson and the organist—and with much greater care than is often the case. The time and thought which invariably underlines the Free Church choice of hymns is something we in the C. of E. might generally emulate to advantage.

Two successive hymns in the same key or metre, too many hymns with eight-line verses and the excessive repetition of well-worn favourites should be avoided. Often an analysis of hymns sung during the year will reveal 'favourites' sung more often than others, many of which may echo shaky theology and which, through familiarity, are probably sung without much thought.

Most services contain too many hymns. This can easily result in an indigestible diet, especially if they are crowded in willy-nilly, either to fill up otherwise awkward gaps or because it is assumed that the people *want* a lot of hymns. How daunting it is to see four, or even five, numbers on the hymnboard, with perhaps a sixth pinned on to the bottom for good measure at festivals.

Silence in worship is a rare virtue!

If parson and organist can, by mutual consent, agree over the controversies of 'pop' (twentieth-century hymns?) and choruses, so much the better. Even some of the clergy most avid in advancing what they foresaw as the merits of these types of hymns are now realising how poor, dull and ephemeral many of them are. As in all artistic endeavour, taste and time ultimately sift out the dross. It must surely always be a question of what is worthy. This matters very much, despite what some clergy would have us believe to the contrary.

Into the same category come hymns for children, of which the Standard Edition of *Hymns Ancient and Modern* and *Songs of Praise* have perhaps the lion's share. Whether children specifically need hymns which are superseded at a certain age by 'grown-up' examples is questionable. Many hymns surely speak to all age groups, the best of the redoubtable Mrs Alexander being a case in point.

Without a choir it is best to avoid certain unfamiliar hymns, unless there is some kind of rehearsal. A congregation on its own needs a greater (though not excessive) volume of organ support than when a choir is present. *Pianissimo* 'verses are generally unsuitable for congregation alone.

If the parson does decide to choose the hymns on his own, he ought to do this well in advance so that the choir have time to prepare them. It is grossly unfair for hymns to be given to an organist on a Saturday evening, especially if the list contains some less familiar ones.

A number of helpful books have been written on hymnody. Some of those specially recommended are listed in Appendix 7.

The choice and number of hymns

Holy Communion. To start off with the right type of hymn can effectively set the pace of a service. Its initial impact can even be responsible for much of the ensuing success of the service. A bright and rhythmic introit-type hymn, such as *Come, let us join our cheerful songs, Let all the world in every corner sing* or *Firmly I believe and truly* will, without fail, produce a positive effect, provided it is sung and played with energy and vitality.

By contrast, the Gradual (between the Epistle and Gospel) calls for something gentler and more reflective, such as *O Holy Spirit, Lord of grace, Blest are the pure in heart* or *Be thou my guardian and my guide.* Alternatively, a short portion of psalmody or a quiet motet for the choir is eminently suitable at this point as a flexible variant.

At the Offertory more substance is called for. A broad and expansive hymn, such as *Ye watchers and ye holy ones, Glorious things of thee are spoken* or *Praise to the Holiest in the height* is of the right length, each having enough verses to take care of the Offertory itself and the preparation of the elements. Even if the Celebrant is ready to go on with the service before the hymn has ended, this should never be made an off-the-cuff excuse for prematurely ending the hymn, the more so as the final verse is usually the climax of the hymn and as necessary to the story as the last act of a play. *When I survey the wondrous Cross* is but one obvious example of a hymn which cumulatively builds up to the last verse and without which it goes out like a damp squib.

During the Administration both congregation and choir are primarily concerned with the mechanics of getting to and from the altar. Under such circumstances hymnody is usually less than satisfactory and should never be used as a means of covering up movement from one part of the church to another. It is more to the point for the choir to sing something on their own before or after the people communicate. A less familiar, or un-congregational hymn, such as *Jesu, meek and gentle, O King enthroned on high* or well-known words to a new or unknown tune can prove a meaningful addition to the service. A carefully chosen anthem at this juncture can be equally suitable for resouceful choirs. Whatever music is sung—or played on the organ—it becomes more effective when followed by silence rather than the inevitable organ meander.

Whether the final hymn follows the communion of the people or comes at the end of the service matters far less than the choice of something big in sound and dimension. Whether it be a seasonal hymn or one of thanksgiving, this is the point in the service for something reasonably short, yet long enough for the Ablutions. *Now thank we all our God, Praise to the Lord, the Almighty, the King of creation* or *Ye holy angels bright* spring to mind as being suitable. At whatever point in the service the hymns may be used, the choice is limitless and what have been suggested here are but a few, chosen—but carefully chosen—at random.

Mattins and Evensong. Should there by a hymn at the start? Some people feel *very* strongly on the matter, the first response being cited as demanding a preceding musical silence. Our mouths having been previously opened in spoken penitence is one thing, while a service beginning with 'O Lord open thou our lips' is another proposition.

If there is to be a hymn at the start, then a robust example is called for, as in the Eucharist. A short 'general' hymn such as *Awake, my soul, and with the sun* or *Ye servants of God, your Master proclaim* will readily set the scene.

At Evensong, the Office Hymn is an admirable custom which has considerable point if sung after the first lesson and therefore immediately before *Magnificat*. A Saint's Day or other specific occasion in the Church's Year can thus be marked to advantage. *The English Hymnal* is particularly rich in providing ideas for what can be used here.

Bearing in mind the tendency to overload a service with hymns, there is much to be said for linking the Collects with any Occasional Prayers or other Intercessions and thus dispensing with a hymn after the Third Collect, especially if there is a sermon with yet a further hymn to follow. An anthem after the Third Collect is another matter, for it breaks up the succession of hymnody and adds a desirable element of variety.

The range of hymns and hymn books, old and new, is legion. Viewed as a whole and bearing in mind the choice available for any one occasion, it is the more surprising how narrow and repetitive a range of hymns persists in so many churches. Conservatism in the pews and 'the congregation won't know it' are always quoted as the excuse. But, whatever may be the cause, it emphasises a lack of vision and awareness for what can, and should, be an important part of evangelism.

The choice of hymn book

Exciting things have been happening in hymnody during the past few years. A growing awareness of needs, coupled with a critical appraisal of some dubious examples of the past hundred years, is offset by an equally growing awareness of what is relevant in terms of today.

The main books in use in Anglican circles are:

Hymns Ancient and Modern. The standard edition, with blue covers, has a dull and forbidding typography and design which is reflected in some of its contents. Even so, it still retains a degree of unquestioning popularity, especially in conservative areas.

The Revised edition (published in 1950) is a different proposition, both in looks and in content. It cut out some of the dead wood or 'the putrefying matter', as someone recently described it, of the Standard Edition. The 1950 edition can hardly claim to be a pioneering book, but it gathers together material which has come to be widely acceptable during this century. It probably contains a higher proportion of singable material than any other book, and it cuts across any party divisions.

The 1950 edition can, without qualification, be recommended as the best and most suitable all round book for average parish use. It is probably the most widely used hymn book at the present time.

100 Hymns for Today, first published in 1969 as a supplement to A & M Revised, was the first significant breakthrough in terms of a contemporary outlook in hymnody. It contains many fine examples, especially in the words which emphasise a strong and positive theology. Its almost astronomical sales indicate how widely the book is used, and its distinctive red, white and blue cover is a familiar landmark in many a church here and overseas.

More Hymns for Today is the second supplement of one hundred hymns to be published by Hymns Ancient and Modern. It includes many of the finest examples of the past decade, not least in words. There are a number of hymns dealing with the Holy Spirit, an area curiously deficient in most of the standard books. Published in 1980, it has been widely acclaimed. Its cover design is identical to its predecessor but coloured green and yellow for easy identification.

Songs of Praise is a well-intentioned child of its time, and little more. It contains some worthwhile examples, but not enough to justify this strangely assorted and doctrinaire collection, much of which is overpoweringly nationalistic in flavour. Although it has a certain popularity in schools, the section 'For Children' is, in its sentiments and language, already hopelessly dated.

The English Hymnal numbers among its admirable contents a wide and useful choice of Communion and Saints Day hymns. These are complemented by some fine early tunes and words coming from Europe. It is unfortunate that this widely ranging all-purpose book, even if slightly specialist, should have been labelled 'High Church', perhaps because of the inclusion of a number of plainsong tunes.

Canon Cyril Taylor, in writing about *The English Hymnal,* says 'it presupposes a more musically cultured and liturgically conscious public than A and M, and a good deal of its material is therefore unlikely to be used in the average church'.

It is surprising that *The English Hymnal Service Book,* published in 1962, has not appealed more. Within its covers are 298 hymns, the words of which are in the parent book. The canticles and all 150 psalms appear in a neatly pointed and easily readable version, together with the Versicles and Responses for Mattins and Evensong and Merbecke's Communion Service music.

Perhaps it appeared just that bit too soon in advance of the impact of the Liturgical Movement on the parish churches of England for it to have the circulation it deserves, for its contents have now largely been superseded in the light of events.

The RSCM's supplement, *Hymns for Celebration,* contains 28 examples of Communion hymns, many of which had not appeared before in print. They represent most denominations and are suitable also for general use.

Oxford University Press, as the publishers of *The English Hymnal,* have now joined the supplement band-wagon with *English Praise.* Among its hundred or more items, together with some comparatively recent hymns, are a number already well proven elsewhere. As with *The English Hymnal Service Book,* this supplement also contains some carols and a small section of responsorial psalms.

The Cambridge Hymnal, which appeared in 1967, is a realistic attempt at coming to terms with the needs of schools. While it does not set out to cater for the congregational market as such, it should not be overlooked in this respect, even if some of the contents tend to make it something of an anthem book. Elizabeth Poston was its musical editor and there is much to be gleaned from this book as Leonard Blake, writing in *English Church Music 1968,* quickly saw: 'Everybody concerned with the habitual, institutional use of hymns should study it; and church musicians should be grateful for its provocation, its buoyant break with stuffiness, and its clarion call to truth in our church praise. Whether it will ultimately rank among the hymn books of seminal influence can be left to the judgement of later generations.'

The *Anglican Hymn Book* (1965) is a generous collection of nearly 700 examples, among which is much new music. In company with other newish hymn books, it includes some commendable arrangements for resourceful choirs. Some original descants and a remarkably good Christmas section add to the overall interest.

The tenth anniversary of its first publication was marked by a new edition containing a supplement of 49 additional tunes, many of them newly composed. A thematic guide has also been published for use in conjunction with the book, while the original edition contains a metrical index complete with musical examples.

With One Voice, subtitled 'A Hymn Book for All the Churches,' was published by Collins in 1979. Its wide-ranging contents—579 examples in all—have proved a useful addition to what is currently available. It first appeared in 1977 as *The Australian Hymn Book,* where it included a Catholic supplement of 44 hymns.

Cantate Domino, published on behalf of the World Council of Churches, is ecumenical in the broadest of terms. With a text printed in many languages (the underlying principle being to present each hymn in its original tongue) and a musical content embracing an equally wide range of globe-spanning interest, a book such as this could well be a pointer towards the shape of things to come. The one drawback is the price which, even in terms of today, is preposterously expensive.

Finally, and as with the previous examples discussed, in no particular order of preference, comes *Hymns for Church and School.* Now twelve years old, this successor to the *Public Schools Hymnbook* will repay careful scrutiny, for it contains examples which can be put to effective use in a variety of circumstances, in or out of school.

On the so-called 'pop' or 'twentieth-century' hymn front there are collections in profusion, ranging from the glossy covered books put out by Galliard and Weinberger to the more substantial volumes of *Youth Praise.* It is difficult to evaluate such hymns without appearing to be dog-in-the-manger or establishment minded. As the 'pop' element in secular music is very much conditioned to an ephemeral approach there seems little reason to doubt that parallel efforts in church music will be subject to a similar life span.

Despite all we hear to the contrary, the average churchgoer is as basically conservative over his music as he is over most other aspects of church life. This, coupled with the triviality, both in words and music, of so much 'pop', only strengthens the view that there is little of lasting value compared with the best of what has survived the centuries. In any event, many modern examples are not strictly hymns but choruses.

The one convincing exception to all this is Sydney Carter, whose admirable texts, often with a sting in the tail (I'll live in you, if you'll live in me) are allied to intriguing music. The particular type of folk song style which Sydney Carter has so admirably cultivated seems to have a more natural affinity with the spirit of the liturgy than most of the other 'popular' composers who try their hand at hymnody.

There is much to be said for drawing on the widest possible range of available material. For example, Parry's *Rustington* (AMR 292 i) is a very acceptable alternative to Martin Shaw's *Marching,* a tune almost exclusively associated nowadays with *Through the night of doubt and sorrow.* Similarly, the English Hymnal harmonies (519) for *Ye watchers and ye holy ones* are a much better proposition than those in AMR 602.

An exhaustive survey of the new books and supplements coming in such profusion from almost every denomination will reveal many instances of exciting words and music which can on occasion be used to advantage by Anglicans. Free Church hymnody today is particularly rich in well-informed scholarship and vision. It tells a very different tale from a century ago.

Financial benefits when introducing new hymn books

The Proprietors of *Hymns Ancient and Modern* allow a substantial initial discount to churches about to introduce either edition of the book, *100 Hymns for Today* or *More Hymns for Today*. Applications for such a grant must be made direct to the publishers, Hymns Ancient and Modern Ltd, St Mary's Works, St. Mary's Plain, Norwich NR3 3BH.

Oxford University Press operate a similar Grant Scheme covering no less than seventeen of their publications. *The English Hymnal, Songs of Praise, The BBC Hymn Book* and *The Oxford Book of Carols* are among these. Orders may be sent direct to OUP at Ely House, 37 Dover Street, London W1X 4AH. Where schools requisition through their Local Authority or bookseller, they will not be deprived of a concession so long as the order is clearly endorsed '25 per cent free grant is claimed'. The grant is calculated on a one in four basis and, to obtain maximum benefit, orders should be in multiples of four.

PSALMS

Is psalm singing a congregational pursuit?

It is indisputable that while the singing of psalms is difficult enough for a choir, it is considerably more so for a congregation which is probably expected to sing from an unpointed Prayer Book and to cope with prose containing 'verses' of different lengths. This contrasts with the comparative ease of the metrical rhyming in hymnody. There is also a confusing variety of psalters in circulation, each pursuing its own party line and with widely differing approaches to the subject.

Some of the pros and cons of the main psalters currently in use were dealt with on pages 25–31.

The psalms are laid down in the Lectionary by authority and therefore the choice should not strictly lie with the parson. In practice, however, the clergy frequently make their own choice. In any case there is need for a much more visionary use of the contents of the Psalter. Given that some psalms, such as 58, much of 109 and certain 'cursing' verses, are unsuitable for modern use, there still remains a wide choice, of which only a handful are in general use in many churches.

The Lectionary (SPCK/Mowbray) is something of a guide in this respect, for the division of the Psalter into thirty mornings and evenings is only arbitrary. A glance also at the lectionaries in a number of the new overseas Prayer Books will provide other useful ideas on the subject.

Psalmody, if used imaginatively, can have a valid and meaningful contemporary role, not least in the ASB forms of the Eucharist.

(Chants were discussed on pages 28 and 29.)

Apart from the familiar canticles—and even here the different types of pointing in current use make a unanimity of approach virtually impossible—it must be conceded that psalm singing is not generally a congregational pursuit. Nevertheless, well-intentioned clergy persist in it, often with embarrassing results. If only psalms were more frequently said (but in a natural and intelligent voice) or an efficient choir be allowed to sing them on their own, a more worthy end-product might be possible.

Note: For churches first introducing *The Parish Psalter,* the publishers give two additional free copies for every complete dozen ordered. Application must be made direct to the Addington Press, Addington Palace, Croydon CR9 5AD.

ANTHEMS

The value of the anthem as a means for the choir to shine *in its own right* has been mentioned elsewhere (page 31). The necessity for this cannot be over-emphasised.

The ultimate choice of anthems is so wide that any attempt at naming individual examples would be a daunting and probably not very helpful task. Nor are matters helped by the rate at which music moves in and out of print these days. Suffice it to say that all degrees of difficulty are catered for. The world is therefore your oyster and what matters is the discovery of what is available and how to relate each example to the expertise of an individual choir. There is no doubt that many choirs with slender resources tackle music which is both technically and artistically beyond them.

When a set of loose copies is purchased—and these can be frighteningly expensive these days—there is much to be said for keeping them in plastic folders such as the RSCM produce. This certainly prolongs their life.

THE SERVICES (BOOK OF COMMON PRAYER)

(The ASB will be dealt with in Chapter 4.)

The Eucharist

In those parishes, as distinct from cathedrals, where 1662 or Rite B is in use, the musical content will generally be either minimal or elaborate.

For the former, the ever faithful Merbecke is more than likely to be used. Everyone will feel 'safe' with it. Although frequently ironed out into an *ersatz* type of plainsong far removed from the measured notation Merbecke was at pains to emphasise, it would be very difficult to attempt any serious reform. A diversity of musical interpretations is now firmly embedded into each and every parish, according to the particular whim of the organist or parson concerned. A study of *The Office of the Holy Communion as set by John Merbecke,* beautifully produced by Oxford in 1949 as a limited edition, is particularly revealing in this respect.

There are a number of editions of Merbecke, each at variance with the other and equally hotly contested or decried by self-appointed scholars. The main versions, each with their distinctive approach to the problem of accompaniment, are by:

Royle Shore (published by Novello)*
Eric Hunt and Gerald Knight (published by SPCK)*
Sydney Nicholson (published by Faith Press) and
J. H. Arnold (published by OUP).

Quite apart form Merbecke, other simple and understandably popular settings include Nicholson in G, Harris in F and the two settings by Martin Shaw, the *Anglican Folk Mass* and the *Modal Setting.**

With the increasing use of the ASB, these settings tend to be ousted by the new versions being written.

The more recent setting by Kenneth Leighton (Church Music Society and OUP) can be sung either in unison or in four-part harmony. The music interprets the splendour of the text in no uncertain way and is exciting to sing, not least in the striding Creed with its march-like and positive onwards movement. Musically, this underlines the mood of the Church triumphant on the move. The one drawback is that the organ accompaniment is rather more difficult than the vocal writing.

Mattins and Evensong

Although both services are virtually identical in form, Mattins invariably seems to present problems not found in Evensong, which usually moves along much more easily and

*Now out of print.

with far more 'go'. Whatever reasons there may be for this (perhaps one being the time of the day), the amount of psalmody in Mattins must be a contributory factor. *Venite,* especially if it is sung in full, together with a psalm, *Te Deum* and *Benedictus,* relieved only by two lessons, adds up to a lot of singing which can prove monotonous in the extreme when sung throughout, as so often happens, to Anglican chants.

As mentioned earlier, any self-respecting choir needs to play its own independent role from time to time. Quite apart from anthems, settings of the Canticles can in certain circumstances not only add musical interest but also heighten the impact of a service and help provide a sense of occasion. Nor need it be a matter of 'either or'. *Magnificat* sung as an extended musical setting by the choir alone can be effectively contrasted by *Nunc Dimittis* sung by all to a chant—or *vice versa.*

Responses

For general purposes the simple Ferial version, although perhaps restrictive in musical terms, is probably the most widely used. The responses can be sung, with or without organ, either in four-part harmony or in unison. In most parishes these are sung with an unvarying sameness, Sunday by Sunday. Some imagination, even in churches with slender musical resources, could provide variation. For example, the harmonised version, either played on the organ or accompanied by the choir, could sometimes be contrasted by a bold unaccompanied unison.

The Litany

This wholly admirable feature of *The Book of Common Prayer* has been virtually obliterated in contemporary churchgoing, but it is encouraging to see it included with *The Alternative Service Book 1980.*

A said Litany can be excessively dull, but if sung, and with careful pruning, it can be both effective and meaningful. It is best sung in procession and is especially purposeful (in or out of church) at Rogationtide.

However it is used, and bearing in mind its present day unfamiliarity, the choir and congregation need to be fully informed in advance of its significance, and why it is being used.

The music of Cranmer's Litany was originally sung in unison. A number of harmonised versions are in existence, ranging from Stainer's pedestrian arrangement in *The Cathedral Prayer Book* of 1891 to the admirable setting published by the Church Music Society. There is also an effective plainsong version in the original Briggs and Frere *Manual of Plainsong,* which also appears in the more recent Novello edition edited by J. H. Arnold.

Weddings and funerals

The reasoning which dictates that those to be married should be allowed the music of their choice has probably led to excesses stranger than in any other department of church music. The fact that non-churchgoers use a church merely for respectable convenience means that they have little or no idea of what is suitable. Even more deplorable is the parson who permits inappropriate music, whatever his reasons, and probably without consulting his organist.

Hymns are often chosen on the strength of the first verse, whereas succeeding verses can be singularly inappropriate. The fact that those concerned want a certain hymn because they happen to know it is neither here nor there.

As the Prayer Book permits a choice of psalms, it seems strange that clergy depart from these. The use of metrical psalms is, incidentally, entirely unauthorised.

Much of the music chosen for funerals is coloured by a morbid undercurrent rather than with what the Christian faith is fundamentally concerned with. For example, the inclusion of *Nunc Dimittis* is inappropriate even if the first verse does not appear so.

It is an encouraging sign that memorial services are now more likely to put the emphasis on thanksgiving for the life just completed, and with a more positive choice of hymns and organ music in evidence.

The reading of the introductory Burial Sentences to a background of soft organ music is a theatrical effect which would be better dispensed with.

Carol and other occasional services

What began as the Service of Nine Lessons and Carols at Christmas has now been adapted, and often to advantage, for almost every conceivable festival. Its basic form makes it appropriate and flexible, providing the music marries up to the readings and complements them. The variety of permutations here is endless, as is the choice of available music.

In all parishes, specially devised services are from time to time called for. These can range from Mothers' Union or Boy Scouts to Rotary and Morris Dancers. Much care is called for in devising such services. (A helpful book is Lawrence Jackson's *Services for Special Occasions,* Mowbray, 1982.) A hymn sandwich may provide an easy, if inappropriate solution. Whatever finally emerges, it must necessarily basically hinge on suitable words linked with equally suitable music. Consultation, with joint planning and rehearsal by *all* concerned, is essential. If a choir is to be employed, a carefully chosen anthem can add to the sense of occasion and provide an opportunity for music in its own right.

Unlike the regular Sunday services, each special service is on a 'one-off' basis. The fact that it will probably be attended mostly by people who otherwise seldom go to church means that they will be watching and listening in a novel and quizzical way, and that they are likely therefore to be critical.

There is a constant need to remember that each church and each service calls for its own set of circumstances. What works in one church will not automatically come off in another.

FURTHER POINTS

Bell ringers

Even if everyone living within earshot of a church cannot escape hearing the sound of church bells (which, after all, is the object of this particular exercise), the few minutes before a service commences is another matter.

For those sitting in the body of a church, the mixture of loud bells in one key and soft organ music in another is a cacophony calculated to offend even the most unmusical. Nor is it likely to act as setting the mood for the service, which is what the organ music should do.

It is surely possible for the bell ringers to be asked to finish five minutes before the service starts, so that the organist can take over.

The end of a service, especially if it be a wedding or 'state' occasion, is another matter, if only for the fact that the organist will be playing a loud voluntary and everyone is feeling fully festive.

Service lists

Although details of hymns and other music, including organ voluntaries, are frequently published in the parish magazine or in a weekly bulletin, a list in the church porch is informative and readily accessible. It is helpful to the regular worshipper and of interest to the casual visitor.

Some of the more enlightened parish magazines devote space to occasional articles on music. This is an example of a public relations exercise and will be much appreciated.

Local schools – what to do when they come to church

When local schools come to church, it must be realised that much that goes on is from the outset suspect and incomprehensible to those on the receiving end, unless they have been properly instructed. A carefully planned service—in consul-

tation with the school—can help to dispel any such misunder-
standings.

As the hymns sung in schools nowadays tend towards the
'pop' chorus type, it is sensible to include a couple of these on
such an occasion. It might also be suggested that the school
learn a traditional type hymn, but one with a compelling
rhythm and good tune. 'Let all the world' to Harwood's fine
tune *Luckington,* 'Firmly I believe and truly' to *Halton
Holgate,* 'Ye holy angels bright' to *Darwall's 148th* and any
of the words associated with Cyril Taylor's fine tune *Abbot's
Leigh* are but four random examples.

The school orchestra might be usefully employed either to
help, together with organ and/or piano, in the accompaniment of the hymns or in its own right, preferably by playing
something during the course of the service. The beginning
and end of the service are not good moments as movement
and talking distract attention.

Pastoral possibilities of a useful kind exist on these
occasions and, who knows, it might spark off a wish to join a
choir or to serve the Church in some other way.

GENERAL INFORMATION JOINTLY CONCERNING PARSON AND ORGANIST

Readers

Much of the role of a Reader, in terms of the conduct of a
service, the choice of music, and relationships with the
musicians, is identical with that of the parson. Where it
differs is in its application. The Reader is frequently a
transient person called on to officiate at a variety of churches
or to assist a parish priest. This calls for an especially tactful
approach as any criticism directed towards the musical
quarter could be interpreted as unwarranted interference.

A Reader does invaluable work and needs just as much
musical encouragement as the incumbent, the more so

perhaps if he/she is not an instinctive singer or a musician. He/she need not feel at a disadvantage, for much of what has already been said in these pages applies with equal validity to the Reader as to the parson.

The RSCM publish a useful 30-page guide for Readers. Entitled *Decently and in Order* and written by Canon Horace Spence, at one time RSCM Clerical Commissioner, it has proved a valuable little book and is in much demand. In fact, some Dioceses automatically arm their new Readers with a copy. It deals with virtually every aspect of the Reader's work in the Lay Ministry, from hints on the use of the voice to detailed help on the services.

There is also an annual course at Addington for Readers. Staffed by those with a perceptive knowledge of the subject, the time-table is both comprehensive and exhaustive.

Links with other churches

Musical links, whether at church choir or choral society level, are valuable exercises, with highly desirable pastoral overtones within the ecumenical framework. The position of the Anglican parish church organist in the community generally makes him/her especially suitable as a leader in this respect.

While the Week of Prayer for Christian Unity is an obvious platform for combined choirs, a Sunday evening service or recital involving joint choirs is no less relevant. There are many permutations depending on the resources of any given area.

Recitals

However desirable recitals are for a choir with the necessary resources, they must from the outset be envisaged as extras. Preparation for a recital should be looked on as an extra commitment, never intruding on the routine week by week choir practice, however tempting this may be.

Christmas provides an obvious opportunity for a carol

concert as distinct from any carol service. If a local instrumental group or school orchestra can be included, so much the better. Most of the ingenious carol arrangements of John Rutter (published by OUP) are not only attractively scored for orchestra, but are within the technical range of many amateur players. They are also highly attractive as music and rewarding both to play and sing.

For Passiontide and Easter, small-scale cantatas such as Charles Wood's *St Mark Passion,* Somervell's *Passion of Christ* and Handel's *The Passion of Christ* (1716) edited by Denys Darlow (OUP) are to be recommended.

On appropriate occasions a recital can provide a useful alternative to Evensong. If carefully devised in conjunction with the parish clergy, its impact can be considerable, especially if the singing is interspersed with suitable readings, biblical or otherwise.

The length and content of a recital need to be carefully worked out and not determined by the enthusiasm of those performers who might wish to present their entire repertoire in one evening. Bearing in mind that the listeners will probably be subjected to hard seats, the inclusion of a hymn gives a welcome opportunity to stretch the legs.

It is much better that the audience go away wanting more rather than vowing never to come back again because the programme was of excessive length. Church conditions can hardly be compared to the atmosphere—and warmth—of the concert hall.

Affiliation to the National Federation of Music Societies, 1 Montague Street, London WC1B 5BS provides choral societies and orchestras with the right to apply for a grant towards the cost of promoting concerts. Vocal scores and orchestral parts can also be loaned from member societies.

Publicity

This can often be a weak spot. Dealt with in a half-hearted and spasmodic way, it is merely a waste of money with little hope of a realistic return. Much thought needs to be given to ways and means of finding the maximum return for the minimum of expenditure, or for no expenditure at all.

The parish magazine ought ideally to have a special section, however small, for musical matters. Attractively designed notices, in or out of church, can also do much to help. It is generally not difficult to find a willing art student ready to turn his or her hand to producing something eye-catching.

Advertisements in the press are expensive, especially if 'displayed', and seldom bring a realistic return for the money spent. Local papers are often willing to mention events connected with the church if space is available, especially if the information supplied is reasonably brief and does not need to be rewritten by a sub-editor. This also applies to local radio stations who will generally be very helpful, the more so if the particular news item has an unusual slant to it.

The essential criteria are to let the public know what you have to offer, to remember that advertising is a subtle and powerful factor in contemporary communication, and to be sure that preparation of handbills and programmes is not left to the last minute.

When all is said and done, never forget that personal word-of-mouth recommendation from the performers themselves will be the best medium for attracting your audience.

Seeking help

As with advertising, take every opportunity of getting help to increase efficiency within a parish environment. Without this it is easy to become insular.

The RSCM, for example, is in business to help and encourage, yet the extent of the benefits of affiliation is not always fully realised, even by some of the paid-up members. These benefits are set out in Appendix 2.

Flower festivals

As an occasional event, this new vogue in church life has assumed significance both from an artistic point of view and as a money spinner. Mini-recitals, either by the choir or organist, are a much appreciated extra. If the day is carefully planned, the recitals can be slotted into the programme as short periods of up to ten minutes at a time, during which people can sit down, look at flowers and listen to music. Such occasions are a useful opportunity for the musicians to do something away from the familiar context of the church service. They provide a personalised contribution to the sense of occasion and the chances are that they will be heard by a wider audience than usual.

Broadcasting

If your church is asked to broadcast, resist the temptation to fire all your big musical guns. It is understandable that both choir and organist will want to make the most of the occasion but be careful not to bite off more than you can chew.

If it is to be a televised service a long anthem will probably be ruled out by the producer. Three or four minutes is a long time in terms of television, much too long for exclusive pictures of a choir and organist. By contrast, the impact of a simple short anthem can be quite something. Note this next time you are watching a televised service.

A physical consideration is the length of rehearsal time necessary before the transmission. Both in terms of singing and the inevitable waiting around, this can be very exhausting for the choir especially if it is for television when poweful lighting adds to the fatigue.

All these remarks apply equally to the parson in connection with his own specific role.

4

The Musical Issues of The Alternative Service Book 1980

Let us be clear that musical issues cannot be viewed as distinct from, or separate from, liturgical considerations. For the first time since the seventeenth century we have new services in the Anglican Church which need new music. How challenging this is for the musician and how retrograde, even cowardly, to attempt to adapt the old music.

Everyone connected with the Church today is aware that it is an age of great liturgical change. The feeling of communication and togetherness stimulates many people, although some find the language bewildering.

In a liturgical sense so much has happened so quickly that composers have been slow to grasp the opportunities. Their reluctance could be because for some the text of the ASB presents neither stimulus nor inspiration. Whatever the reason, what has been produced so far represents a very small cross-section of professional composers compared with the number of amateur composers who have come up with settings of Holy Communion Rites A and B. What significance, if any, attaches to this?

Although this section is concerned with recent Church of England liturgies, I hope that what I have to say will be seen in the context of other new liturgies within the Anglican Communion. Nearly all of these have some common ground with Rites A and B, or these services to theirs. It would therefore be unrealistic, and dishonest, to suggest that what has emerged in England as the result of the Liturgical Commission's work over the past twenty years is the sole criteria, for its influence is far-reaching. A study of Colin Buchanan's *Modern Anglican Liturgies 1958-68* and his *Further Anglican Liturgies 1968-75* (Grove Books) shows what has been happening in many parts of the world.

RITE B (formerly Series 1 and 2 Revised)

Holy Communion

When the service first appeared as Series 2 in 1967 it was, apart from what was officially the 'unauthorised' Prayer Book of 1928, the first radical change since 1662. Even so, the revisions affected the music only marginally. These can be quickly summarised:

1 In *Gloria in excelsis* the repeated phrase 'Thou that takest away the sins of the world, have mercy upon us' was dispensed with.

2 In the Creed, the catholic and apostolic Church became 'one *Holy* catholic . . .' (as in 1928).

3 *Benedictus* may *either* follow *Sanctus, or* may come at the end of the Prayer. As *Sanctus* now became part of a continuous prayer, the *Amen* at its conclusion was omitted.

4 Two words were altered in the *Our Father.* As both remained words of one syllable no musical problem arose for those churches which sang the Lord's Prayer.

Some musicians, mainly in cathedrals where more elaborate settings were used than in the majority of parish churches, made appropriate changes in the existing music. Usually it transpired that things were left as they were with the music sung as before. As the textual changes were so minimal this was probably the wisest course.

Morning and Evening Prayer

The changes here were:

1 In the opening set of versicles and responses, the *Gloria* became one continuous sentence, either spoken or sung by 'Minister and People'.

2 In the *Gloria* at the end of the canticles and psalms 'Holy Ghost' became 'Holy Spirit'.

3 'Sabaoth' in *Te Deum* now became 'Hosts'.

4 The penultimate response before the Collects was the one new departure, becoming 'For it is thou, Lord, only who makest us dwell in safety'.

In terms of the music, these alterations were again so minimal that they were either ignored or easily overcome.

It is interesting to see that the canticles now appear in a simple pointed version for singing, while a subsequent edition of the text of the Series 2 Holy Communion (AS 225) included 'the melody of Merbecke'.

The inclusion of pointed psalmody was a significant move towards the now almost universal practice adopted when new services and versions of the psalms are published.

Other Series 2 services, such as Baptism and Confirmation, do not affect the music as such.

Appendix 8 lists some of the published Commentaries on Series 2. See also the companion volume to this present work, *A Handbook of Parish Worship* (Michael Perry).

THE NEXT MOVE—RITE A (formerly Series 3 Revised)

The pros and cons here have probably been more hotly debated than has anything else in living memory within the entire spectrum of the Church. This is true for the clergy as much as the man and woman in the pew and the shouting has by no means died down. In fact, it has provoked something of a revolution – and how good for us all to be shaken by the roots and made to think about our worship in the 1980s. It certainly was not always thus.

What has happened affects virtually every worshipper, for each denomination is, in its own way, being subjected to many changes. Our changes within the Church of England are small compared with that of the Church of Rome where baby, bath water, bath and all have been thrown out. We at least have retained our vernacular, even if it has not been modernised to everyone's liking.

But we must always remember that what has taken place is against the background of the conservatism for which the Church and its people are renowned. What is familiar is safe and therefore presents no threat.

Series 3 and Rite A Holy Communion have exploded the priestly monopoly of 1662 and provided in its place a part for all to play, with special emphasis on communication and togetherness.

How does music fit into this?

Holy Communion

Because the emphasis is laid, and rightly so, on the corporate nature of the Eucharist, most of the settings have either played the music 'in a low key' (both metaphorically and deliberately) or sought to think in terms of a congregation, which sometimes is to the detriment of choirs. When John Rutter's setting appeared (and he was first in the field) musical eyebrows were raised at seeing 'For congregational use with optional SATB choir' boldy printed on the front page.

Although it is interesting to compare the approach of different composers (see for example the settings by Richard Shephard, Peter Aston and Gelineau) the accent has been more on unison settings – within the vocal range of congregations – rather than on the more elaborate cathedral-type versions such as those by Francis Jackson, Bryan Kelly,

Arthur Wills and Philip Moore. Some have been published with separate unison versions on cards for congregational use.

The choice is so wide now that it would be invidious to suggest what to opt for and what to avoid. In any event, some versions had a short lived existence while one must realise that what may be suitable in one parochial situation would be out of place in another. This state of affairs, together with the many permitted deviations and permutations (quite apart from the private amendments some clergy themselves introduce) leaves many people with a feeling of restlessness.

We sometimes tend to forget how recent these new services are. Compared with 300 years of the Book of Common Prayer it is no small wonder that the liturgical sea is still very choppy and will probably continue to be for some time to come.

While it is fully recognised that financial resources must be a determining factor and that the introduction of new music for both choir and congregation can prove very expensive today, I would suggest that churches endeavour to have two contrasted settings in use. A simple version could be for general use and a slightly more elaborate one for festivals. Alternatively, *Gloria* and *Sanctus* could be sung to the simple setting while the choir might be responsible for *Benedictus* and *Agnus Dei*. The type of setting chosen depends on many considerations, not least being the joint needs, attitudes and resources of a particular choir and congregation.

Some composers have provided music for everything that can be sung. As Rite A has been accused of containing too many bits and pieces, churches might consider saying the Acclamations – but doing so in an exciting and realistic way. Rite A has also been accused of eroding away some of the choir's work, seldom giving them a chance to excel. These observations probably have an element of truth in them. They certainly show up some of the problems.

To encourage the choir and give them their head, a short motet or non-congregational hymn might be sung during the Administration. As the attention of the congregation is at this time focussed on the altar and getting there and back, it is surely a good time for the choir to sing on their own.

Peter Aston, Richard Shephard and Bryan Kelly have also set the Seasonal Sentences. The first two, published by the RSCM, are simple but attractive miniatures, Bryan Kelly's are an extended exercise for full choir – and very expensive.

Where there is no choir, suitable organ or even recorded orchestral music might be played during the Administration. This latter I have heard to good effect overseas and at this particular juncture of the service it can be a helpful aid to worship.

As with Series 2, the now familiar service booklets include a version 'with music for the congregation'. Written jointly by Christopher Dearnley and Allan Wicks on lines similar to those adopted by Merbecke in 1550, the music is intended to stand 'half-way between the spontaneous inflexions of ordinary speech and music deliberately composed'. Intended also as something simple enough for any congregation 'to master quickly' its aim is to 'serve the purpose of being a guide for future attempts'. It is therefore the more unfortunate that, on a parochial level, the music has often been found in practice to be too subtle and difficult. Even so, the preface to the booklet (AS 325) is well worth reading.

Finally, two other possible – and permitted – ways exist:

1 A said service with hymns is not to be despised. It can make a most effective contrast to a sung service and there is much to commend in it especially when congregation and choir resources are slender or the latter non-existent.

2 An escape clause in the prefatory notes says 'Where parts of the service are also sung to well-known musical settings, it is permitted to use the words for which these settings were composed'. Which takes us back to square one, 1662 style. And, moreover, it works that way. The sounds of seventeenth and twentieth century languages side by side present no problem or awkwardness when one is said and the other sung.

Appendix 9 lists the main ASB musical versions currently available. The RSCM periodically issue a check list of music in print; this also contains a short note on each setting.

Appendix 10 deals with some of the books and commentaries on the new service.

These Appendices are not intended to be in any way exhaustive.

Morning and Evening Prayer

Although conceived on the basic framework of the familiar 1662 Mattins and Evensong, the net result is very different. This is especially noticeable in language. The services are much shorter and to the point, containing a breath of much needed fresh air.

A new set of canticles now appear, one for each day of the week, the more familiar examples often having a new place and role. As in Series 2 (Rite B), all are pointed for singing but appear in the modern translations referred to earlier.

The versicles and responses, which bear little resemblance to those in the Book of Common Prayer, are now published by the RSCM complete with traditional Ferial tones duly adapted. The Litany appears in a modern version.

Other ASB services

The Funeral Services (ASB 60) are also available. These have no specific musical provision but 'Points are indicated for the singing of hymns'.

How to introduce the ASB

Prior information and consultation at all levels over an extended period of time is the prime necessity. It never pays to rush the introduction of something new into a parish, least of all the ASB, which has to be 'sold'. The odds will be that the congregation, and perhaps the choir and organist, have an inbuilt resistance and resentment for anything unfamiliar. The fear of most churchgoers for something new and untried will be diminished, and may even be turned into willing acceptance, if they understand what it is all about. For these reasons explanation and information are a necessity. See *A Handbook of Parish Worship* (Michael Perry), especially chapter 2.

Any such preparation must obviously be both on a liturgical and musical basis and must include plenty of rehearsal, not least in the preparation. However simple the ceremonial may be, it must be well done.

Having suitably paved the way, the new service should be introduced with a flourish, for first impressions will be the most lasting.

The RSCM will, on request, be glad to assist in promoting workshops for parishes wishing to introduce the ASB. These events not only include help on the musical issues as such, but are planned to be of equal assistance to the clergy and congregation in their respective roles in the new services.

Hints to would-be composers

As already mentioned, the new services have not yet fired either the imagination, or the inspiration, of many top-level composers. Professional musicians have been reluctant to write music because of the experimental nature of the texts. Now that the ASB is a fact of life and here with permanency, it is to be hoped that composers will feel more encouraged to put pen to paper.

It is debatable whether the new text is easier or more difficult to set than 1662. To take a specific example, the lilting metrical rhythm of 'Glory to God in the highest and peace to his people on earth' is, on the face of it, easier to set to music than the 1662 counterpart. But it would be foolish to judge comparative texts on one such sample. Note also, by comparison with 1662, the new punctuation in the Rite A Sanctus which now reads 'Holy, holy, holy Lord . . .' .

It may be of some interest to set out the requirements given by the RSCM to composers asked to set the new text. These include:

1 A considerable amount of unison, either sopranos and altos contrasted with tenors and basses, or all voices in unison.

2 Occasional, and optional, four-part harmony. SAB also desirable because of the shortage of tenors.

3 No division of parts.

4 Compass of voice parts important. For example, avoid anything above G for sopranos or tenors.

5

The Congregation

Relationships between congregations and musicians can often be difficult. A shortsighted and unrealistic organist and choir may look on the congregation as an obstruction to their music-making or, at best, as a necessary evil. On the other hand there are some individuals in a congregation who cannot toe any line at all. They just sing loudly, out of tune and out of time. These are crosses to be borne by *all* concerned and call for very tactful handling. In neither case is there a ready made answer.

It should be understood from the outset that musicians and congregation each have an important yet distinctive role to play, sometimes together and sometimes separately. Today this is rightly emphasised by much of the liturgical reform of recent years. Each party must understand and value the other's contribution. Assuming all concerned wish it, such a valhalla is not difficult to achieve.

Relationships are fundamental yet are the cause of many troubles. The choir which ignores, or plays down, the role of the congregation is treading as dangerous a path as the congregation (probably aided and abetted by the parson) which underplays the particular function and role of the choir.

If, however, there is a good choir and a strong musical tradition, the congregation should value and take pride in it as an important factor in the parish and its worship. Conversely, the musicians should treat the congregation as part of their musical scene, even though their musical function may be restricted to little more than singing hymns.

The moral surely is to get the congregation on the side of the musicians and to involve them – never to alienate them. Thus encouraged, the average congregation often finds it can sing much better than it thought and, as a result, is the more likely to become interested in the music and the musicians. This helps to promote good relationships which can repay handsome dividends. A contented congregation is more likely to support its choir in a practical way, such as when outings or other social functions are being planned, and when music or new robes are needed.

A reasonable degree of consultation between the musicians and the congregation, either directly through the parson and organist or via the PCC, is invaluable. This can only lead towards an increase in efficiency and understanding. Consultation and discussion is vital when any new departures or experimentation are considered which have a common objective. Imagine a situation when the geographical position of choir and congregation is being rethought. A chancel choir cut off from the congregation in the body of the church is familiar. This mixed blessing is more often than not a liability today. It detracts from the communication and togetherness underlying much contemporary liturgical reasoning, and adds to the difficulty when choirs are smaller and less effective or even non-existent. The consequent moving of the altar from the sanctuary into the body of the church, and therefore among the people, has happened in countless parishes.

In this kind of situation the pooling of evidence and opinion from both sides can help to produce a workable solution. At worst it can result in the inevitable British compromise.

How to involve the congregation in their own right

A little imagination will reveal a number of possibilities, each dictated by the resources and traditions of a church.

For example:

1 Verses in hymns can be sung by the congregation alone. This not only provides contrast and variety but gives the congregation a sense of personal involvement. It is good for a choir to have to listen to the congregation who are then, in their turn, the more likely to feel favourably disposed towards hearing the choir.

2 It is always assumed that everyone automatically *wants* to sing. Often singing is wrongly regarded as the person in the pew's only means of expression when worshipping. What of the spoken parts? Even if these were largely ignored in the past, today they play a fundamental part without which the new services are less than credible. Every effort should be made to ensure that the spoken parts of the service as they affect the congregation are audible, articulate and meaningful. This means using a natural voice instead of the all too familiar ecclesiastical drone referred to earlier.

3 From the practical point of view congregational rehearsals are most important. They focus attention on the people in the pews. More of this later.

4 The congregation should be kept fully informed about the work of the choir which, it should be remembered, usually involves much more than one or two Sunday services attended by most people. A congregation can help to publicise the work of their choir and any musical events that are planned. They can also help to find new recruits (this is always a difficult task) and by generally taking an interest in the individual members.

When good relationships exist, the support thus given can be a practical way of saying thank you.

When there is no choir

Without a choir it is self-evident that if the congregation do not sing, there will be no vocal music. Nevertheless, the people can often sing to better effect than at first seems possible, if they are helped on their way. An organist who knows how to 'lead', and can play rhythmically without always being loud, is a tremendous asset. The parson who sings both loudly and erratically is of little help, however well intentioned his efforts. But in this situation a congregation often reveals a completely unexpected 'do it yourself' talent.

It is essential for everyone to sit together, rather than scattered in ones and twos around the church. If the reason is fully explained there is a chance that those concerned might forsake the seat they have always sat in, especially when they hear for themselves the better results.

In churches where the layout is unsuitable, the organ inadequate, or the acoustics discouraging, congregational music – with or without a choir – is unlikely to be good. It is a fact to be accepted.

Some general considerations, choir or no choir

In any worthwhile situation, new music must from time to time be introduced, if only to avoid vain repetition and stagnation. *New* music does not automatically mean twentieth century 'pop'. A glance at the contents of many of the new hymn supplements will reveal a broad spectrum of words and music, much of it stimulating and inspiring.

The best way to introduce new hymns (or ASB music) implies a psychological approach. The surest way of alienating a congregation is to put on a new tune without prior warning. If advance notice is given, with the choir singing the new hymn as an anthem or the organist playing it (during a service), a positive result is much more likely and a suspicious congregation can be won over.

All the recently published hymn books and supplements include the music, either in a melody-only edition or in a full version. Now that so many have been taught to read music the advantages of this are obvious. Even for those who cannot read music, the visual image of the rise and fall of the printed notation is of help.

The same applies even more forcibly to the psalms where, in contrast to the metrical shape of hymn poetry, each verse is of a different length. It is impossible to expect a congregation to sing with any degree of accuracy without a pointed prayer book. While the many different types of psalter now on the market make uniformity difficult to achieve, whichever psalter is used (pages 25-27 list some of these), the pointing can usually be quickly understood, provided it is fully explained and demonstrated in the initial stages.

Congregational chatter is unfortunately prevalent in many churches, especially during the music before a service starts which should help set the mood for what is to follow. Such chatter is extremely distracting to those trying to concentrate on more pertinent matter, and should be left until the coffee party after the service.

CONGREGATIONAL REHEARSALS

The success or failure of these occasions depends on the person taking the rehearsal. If neither the organist nor the parson are able to put it across so as to make the congregation want to sing better, the exercise ought not to be attempted. Most congregations prove reluctant, reticent, even stubborn, if they feel they are being got at in this particular respect. 'We've managed for . . . years and don't want these new-fangled ideas' is a very common attitude of mind. Therefore the personality of whoever is in charge is paramount in deciding whether or not there is to be a second venture.

Assuming the first hurdle has been successfully crossed, a regular rehearsal every two or three months might be aimed at. When should this take place? The Parish Communion is obviously ruled out unless ten minutes or so is earmarked at the start of the service. For many reasons this is not always convenient. Were it not for the demise of Evensong in so many parishes it would probably be more practicable to incorporate such a rehearsal into this service.

Perhaps the best solution is for an occasional rehearsal to take the place of the customary Evensong. We did this when I was organist of Exeter Cathedral and found that it worked well, provided the people sat together at the front of the nave. Having closed off the back rows of chairs they had little option but to sit together at the front. We used a piano and placed it in the centre aisle among the people. This was better than using the distant organ, especially as the piano's percussive quality was more conducive to singing. Finally the choir were given a holiday and the congregation left to get on with it on their own.

We always began with a familiar hymn before moving on to learn a new one. Some of the said parts were also dealt with. After about twenty-five minutes' hard work all that had been rehearsed was incorporated into a specially constructed short service for which the organ was used. In this simple way the congregation found encouragement; they even came to enjoy it and, I suspect, many were as pleased as I was with the results of their efforts. It was inevitable that some regular members stubbornly refused to attend these occasions. Some very lame excuses or belligerent comments were relayed back to me, usually at second or third hand.

6

Overseas

There is always the danger that a book such as this is slanted too much towards the specific needs in Britain. But most of what I have said is as relevant in Hong Kong as in Hemel Hempstead, though with certain local differences. Having travelled to many parts of the world my observations have led me to draw certain conclusions. Not surprisingly, the traditionaly links and affinities are strongest in what can be loosely termed the British Commonwealth. The Anglican church in Europe and the Episcopal church in the United States have to a certain extent been coloured by their geographical position. In the case of Europe, for instance, such churches are tiny oases of Anglican tradition surrounded usually by a largely Roman Catholic, or other denominational environment.

A fundamental problem not always appreciated is the sheer physical distance separating such areas from the mother country. The resulting feeling of isolation is a very real factor which even jet travel has as yet done little to overcome.

The fact is that such countries still look to Britain and its long tradition for a lead, and not only in church matters. This is perhaps less obvious in the emerging countries of Africa than in continents such as Australasia, where much of the way of life is English-orientated in looks, temperament and heritage.

Overseas, great distances often separate towns, each of which have fewer churches than we in Britain, though it is true to say that the distance between Barnstaple and Exeter (40 miles) is as formidable to Devonians as that between Cape Town and Johannesburg (1000 miles) is to South Africans, because the latter take such distances in their stride as part of everyday life.

Nevertheless, there has to be much improvisation, due mainly to a lack of competent organists and choirtrainers. This is less apparent in the larger continents than in the smaller, colonial type countries. The constant shift of population with short-term contracts compared with the 'settlers' of a previous generation, makes for a 'here today and gone tomorrow' situation which affects the continuity of church music as much as that of the congregation.

The open air life with predictably good weather for much of the year encourages outdoor pursuits more than in Britain. This is especially so in schools but people are drawn away from weekend church commitments just as they are by the motor car and five-day week in this country.

Even so, those who are keen and hard working sometimes produce better results than in this country. The Church overseas being in so many respects new and young compared with Britain, there is sometimes a spontaneity and freshness of approach in marked contrast to our firmly entrenched centuries of tradition. This can be seen in a number of ways, most of which concern the people themselves. For example, churches are more widely used for all kinds of parochial pursuits than in Britain. And again little of the British reticence is to be found in such customs as the kiss of Peace.

The Church overseas often seems to flourish best under pressure, either when threatened politically – Zimbabwe and South Africa are salient examples of this – or when surrounded by a non-Anglican, even non-Christian environment.

In common with Britain most of the Anglican churches overseas have in recent years produced new liturgies. Nearly all in some measure owe allegiance to our Series 2 and 3, with which they have much in common. The Liturgy, or *The Book of Common Worship* of the Church of South India influenced considerably the shaping of Series 2 Holy Communion.

Contemporary worship, the role of music and the role of the congregation, together with all the other challenges and issues being so hotly contested here, are just as problematic to the Church overseas.

Organs in overseas countries

Organs in countries with extremes of temperature pose difficulties unknown in Britain. Tropical heat, invariably accompanied by very high humidity, together with the ravages caused by termites, are as much a hazard as extreme coldness in winter.

With a growing international demand for English organs, it is encouraging to learn that most organ builders are more experienced at coping with, and overcoming, such problems than they were a few years ago.

For overseas churches contemplating a British organ, three essential points need bearing in mind:

1 A carefully designed *small* organ, fully equal to the needs of a small church, is to be recommended. It is also much less expensive to transport than a large instrument.

2 Do seek the fullest possible advice before making a decision. Always state your needs and the climatic conditions to which the new organ will be subjected. The Secretary of the Organs Advisory Committee (see page 130), or the RSCM, will be glad to help if they are given the fullest information and background.

3 Never rule out the use of a piano for service work and a record player for voluntaries.

Contacts with travelling British musicians

Each year examiners for the Associated Board of the Royal
Schools of Music will be in most commonwealth countries,
though Australia and Canada are notable exceptions. If any
of these examiners are church musicians try to enlist their
help. Do remember, however, that they will already have a
very full and demanding schedule of examinations and may
be reluctant to give up time on an otherwise free Saturday
afternoon or Sunday. But most are, within reason, willing to
do something, the more so if it can be coupled with some
hospitality.

The RSCM are in constant touch with the Associated
Board and know the movements of examiners. Some long-term
planning can result in a choirs festival or an instructional half
day for choirs and organists. Events such as these conducted
by a British musician are comparatively rare overseas and are
therefore usually the more worthwile. They can certainly be a
valuable exercise.

Opportunities for study when in Britain

For overseas church musicians on leave in Britain there are
opportunities for short-term study at the RSCM's head-
quarters at Addington Palace. A wide variety of courses cater
for most aspects of the organist's and choirtrainer's work.
Many are basically planned as refresher courses and designed
to give a new and searching look to the subject. Those attending
such courses invariably find a whole wealth of new thought
which can then be put to practical use on return from leave.

While some come for an extended working holiday, others
opt to attend the RSCM's Annual Summer School for Overseas
Students. This crash course at Addington, which attracts
students of all ages, not least amateurs, from many parts of
the world, is a comprehensive six week course catering for
most aspects of the church musician's craft.

The British Council, through their overseas offices, will be glad to provide information and advice for church musicians intending to visit Britain to gain help with their church music.

Keeping in touch with new music

It is difficult enough in Britain to be fully informed concerning new music being published and of its suitability to any given situation. This state of affairs is more acute overseas where browsing around the few music shops in the larger cities may, or may not, provide much help.

To be able to study the music oneself is much better than relying on advertisements in musical journals, most of which are nebulous and far from really informative. The RSCM tries to compromise through its quarterly journal *Promoting Church Music* which is sent free to all members. In it a sizeable and fully informative section is devoted to new RSCM publications. The RSCM can also supply other publishers' works through a special department where upwards of 300 anthems and services are kept in constant stock. These can be sent to overseas members either by surface or air mail. The service is generally much quicker, and more reliable, than dealing with the publishers direct.

7

Ordinands

A few years ago most theological colleges tended to view the RSCM merely as a vehicle for helping their ordinands to sing 'O Lord open thou our lips'. That was all right as far as it went, but a more enlightened approach has now meant that music and its implications on worship are treated in greater depth and as a serious part of the parson's work.

Visits which I and others now make to a number of theological colleges are useful both for general discussion and for making the contacts which contribute towards greater all round understanding. These visits reveal widely diverging view points, ranging from the almost excessively musical in outlook to the angry young men anxious to put the world to rights, and with little insight as to the part music could play in this. These latter invariably shout the loudest, perhaps as a cover-up for insecurity and immaturity.

Some automatically play down music, having a preconceived and immovable conviction that *any* music in a *traditional* vein must of necessity be harmful. They consider that *contemporary* 'pop' style is the only way to the musical salvation of the young, for no one else surely matters nowadays! Perhaps this is a cynical over-simplification but the dangers are very real and thoroughly disturbing, even though they may only represent one point of view, and a biased one at that.

For some, the subsequent reality of parochial life, especially if it be the rough and tumble of a tough parish, soon dispels any preconceived ideas about church music, while for others, it reveals unsuspected delights and possibilities.

Would that church music, its implications and the ramifications of the parson-*cum*-organist saga could take its place as part of Post Ordination Training.

If you have an interest in music and find your first parish one where the musical tradition is weak, you will inevitably feel musically and probably spiritually despondent. In such circumstances always encourage, rather than register disapproval. Your choir and organist are probably aware of their shortcomings and will be more embarrassed if they know your own musical background. These are ideal conditions for you to help your organist build up the efficiency, morale, and performance of his choir.

Chapter 1 was devoted to the clergy. Study this as an ordinand *now* but relate it to the forseeable future. In this way you can help to avoid some of the pitfalls to which more established clergy sometimes succumb. Try to see music in its proper perspective. The chances are that good relations with your choir, in or out of church, will reap more dividends both to them and to you pastorally than you realise. Even if you are not musical, do at least try to see their point of view.

In your theological college you and your colleagues will be expected to sing in choir. It matters little what your voice is like, but it will give you some experience of singing in public, which eventually you will have to do – and on your own.

College is a time for liturgical experiment, in which musical experiment should also play its part. It is easier and more practicable to experiment here than in a parish. Always remember that experimentation is a necessary exercise, if only for the sake of knowing what to reject.

Finally, two important, and to my mind essential, musts for any would-be parson:

1 Do seek advice. Never be too proud to ask for musical help from those who know, can help, and want to help. Don't be the type of parson who blindly blunders on, stubbornly by-passing any avenues of help.

2 Never be dull. It is unforgivable, especially in church. Your voice and your facial expression influence the congregation strongly. If you speak in a parsonic and laboured manner devoid of interest, it will soon be realised that you have escaped the drama of, for example, the Eucharist. It will show that you have failed to relay the good news of the Christian message. Younger clergy are sometimes more at fault in this respect than the older ones.

Whatever your age, you will influence and condition the services for better or for worse. *Be natural.*

8

H.M. Forces

Much of what has been said elsewhere in this book applies to the Forces, the distinction being that its application is in a specific environment.

The shifting population of much of Service life contributes towards instability and a lack of continuity. It is therefore harder for parson and organist to work together than in a 'civilian' church. This may have the advantage of avoiding the stagnation brought on by years of unrelieved sameness, although it is also true that to project a personality needs some time for its full effect to be felt. This applies equally to a choirtrainer.

The 'here today and gone tomorrow' philosophy of Service life constitutes a major obstacle met with less often by the more permanently trained choir in a traditional parish environment. Yet bad musical habits seem to be as firmly entrenched in most Forces churches as they are elsewhere.

Although a choir can, through 'the exigencies of the Service' virtually disintegrate and disappear almost overnight, it is surprising how good many of the choirs are. This is especially so overseas where wives (and husbands), together with civilians, often become more involved and have a greater enthusiasm and commitment than here in Britain.

It is to be regretted that our diminishing overseas presence

112 *A Handbook of Parish Music*

means that garrrison churches, many of them long established, have now ceased to function as such. With their passing, a vacuum has been caused and musical links with local civilians in many areas irretrievably severed.

Whatever the situation, Service clergy and musicians, especially those serving overseas, are left very much to their own musical devices.

RSCM links with the forces

For my own part, extended overseas tours as an examiner for the Associated Board of the Royal Schools of Music, and now in my RSCM work, have made me aware of the need to provide help. Through links which have now been forged, I am managing to visit Service choirs both in Britain and over- seas. The creation of such contacts and the provision of practical help to choirs in their own environment has been a new deployment of RSCM facilities which, in its wake, has built up a series of personal links and contacts, especially with the Army.

The world of church music in the Forces being so much smaller than its 'civilian' counterpart means that I now know many chaplains, even if almost every time I meet them it is in a different place.

The RSCM likes to think that any seeds sown in this way will bear fruit when Service musicians return to civilian life. As the demand for organists and choirtrainers far exceeds the supply, an experienced person should find little difficulty in securing a post to his liking. The added experience of a disci- plined Service way of life would, on the face of it, seldom come amiss in most parishes.

For those who are wary concerning religion in the Forces, especially if borne of wartime experiences, it is only fair to say that it is a mistake to think of church music in the Forces as being made up of military bands *ad nauseam*. It is equally misleading to equate the Forces with nothing but sentimental hymns and no place for anything but a centre-of-the-road approach, with a leaning towards 'low Church'.

My one real quarrel is with the Ministry of Defence's apparently almost *de rigueur* obsession with installing electronic organs whenever possible. (See page 49.)

9

Conclusions

LOOKING BACK

At this point I suggest that you re-read the introduction. Then, in the light of the succeeding chapters, let us look back reflectively, drawing certain conclusions which I believe – and believe mightily – to be essential apects of parish music at its best. There are seven of these.

Personal relationships

Probably the most important of all is the matter of personal relationships. When any musical situation within a church breaks down, experience repeatedly shows that in lesser or greater degree it stems from a clash of personalities, clashes which in most instances could have been avoided. This can show itself by opinionated persons in head-on collision or the behaviour of the weak, insecure person whose only line of defence is to exert himself at all costs. It is usually the uncertain person who can so often be objectionable.

Relationships will always be workable if, from the outset, the demarcation lines are clearly drawn, understood and acted on in an unselfish way.

Listen as well as play

Whenever possible put yourselves – both parson and organist – on the receiving end as members of the congregation. Nor should this be confined to musical services. A said Communion service concentrating on words alone can be just as moving an experience as one with all the frills. Musical or not, the chances are that it will prove a salutary experience, probably humbling in the process and certainly very different from what you envisaged (if you ever seriously envisaged it at all) from your position on the giving end in the chancel. Having spent most of my life as an organist I now find myself, more often than not, a member of the congregation. It is an experience both traumatic and revealing.

Linked with all this and perhaps something of a reverse procedure is the old concept of God 'up there', distant in the sanctuary and remote from the worshipping body of the faithful down in the church. Although the emphasis on togetherness created by liturgical changes in recent years has done something to eliminate this separation, music can help to provide a bridge.

Formal worship

When all the shouting about 'being with it', informal, or giving the teenagers what they want, eventually dies down, remember that a formal building such as a church demands formal worship, a process for which it has above all else been set apart in a unique way. With this in mind, honest experimentation is one thing while mere gimmickry can become dishonest manipulation.

In this respect, it could be to our advantage to encourage much more use of talents and the exchange of ideas. An ideal musical situation should surely not depend solely on the parson or the organist who will inevitably run out of steam from time to time. There is always a reserve of credible talent somewhere in the congregation waiting to be tapped.

Encourage all concerned

Do constantly encourage your choir, your congregation, and each other, to strive for high standards in all aspects of worship. The ideal of raising one's sights high and keeping them there is frequently suspect in contemporary society where the lowest common denominator is so often accepted as the panacea for all ills. Look where it has got us.

For the organist and the choirtrainer, do you want to improve your work? Do you know how to go about it? In church circles there is often a fear of change, even a built-in resistance to it, for change is frequently interpreted as decay.

On the other hand, modern opportunities for experiencing excellence are without precedent. The long-playing record, tapes, cassettes, 'live' concerts, broadcasting (and church music is incredibly well represented on the BBC), should prove a stimulus and an objective. Is such perfection a stimulant or does it tend to act in a strange way as a depressant? Informality and excellence are not impossible bedfellows.

Discrimination in church music

Do we want *all* our church and organ music, irrespective of its quality, to be permanent, or are we prepared for some of it to be ephemeral, and therefore expendable? Looking at the repertoire of many a church, much which is revered ought to be dispensed with, and without delay.

New hymns

Did you never make any new friends? New hymns, both in words and music, as with new friends, should be added to old ones, not necessarily becoming substitutes for them.

The organist and the congregation

Think carefully about the congregation and their particular role on their own or jointly with the choir, the latter being in line with present-day liturgical reasoning. Think of those situations where there is no choir and where, by default, the congregation has to cope alone. Think also of those churches where, because the choir is so good and efficient, their music virtually becomes a take-over bid. Sometimes this can happen unintentionally and without a choir realising it. In other instances it can be the carefully calculated policy of an elite who do not see themselves either as part of a liturgical pattern or of a worshipping community.

In this last respect, how desirable it is that the organist and choirtrainer be practising Christians. This does not mean a grudging or reluctant approach to the altar as a communicant, but a sincere desire to see their work as part of the framework of worship. The musician who really believes transmits this through his/her playing and through the choir training. This something, or lack of it, makes itself abundantly clear to those listening and, if positive, can enrich beyond measure. Technical excellence is a desirable attribute, but singing and playing 'with the spirit and with the understanding' is, in the long run, more important.

WARNING SIGNS

Has the liturgical pendulum swung too far towards an over-emphasis, and an over-simplification of togetherness? As the Free Churches become more liturgically minded, are we of the Anglican Church tending to move away from liturgical to non-liturgical, 'do-it-yourself' services? What are the implications, and perhaps the threats, of the growth of the charismatic movement?

Much of this is reflected in a background tending more towards the Evangelical approach, where music is questioned and 'traditional' music is suspect as an aid to worship. The ASB is another factor, even if a subconscious one, which plays down the role of music in terms of the choir.

We live in an age which, for better or for worse, questions virtually everything. The Church, the establishment, and with it the traditions of church music are therefore obvious targets. From the humblest village parish to the grandest cathedral there are today formidable problems and dangers which spring from a set of circumstances which seldom, if ever, exercised the attentions of previous generations. The church music scene is in many practical respects governed by the attitudes – both individual and corporate – of society at large. This means that healthy dialogue, discussion, and sharing in each other's worship, is a twentieth-century manifestation – and a particularly valid one at that – of the Holy Spirit at work within us.

THE CHALLENGE OF THE FUTURE?

Music impresses more than speech. By making provision for the use of music in worship, the Book of Common Prayer showed that it made more meaningful what otherwise would have been spoken. 'Speech beautified' is how Sir Edward Bairstow, that great organist of York Minster, so aptly termed it.

If singing does not fulfil this fundamental criteria, we are failing to promote what music in worship is all about. The human voice is, after all, the only instrument which uses words to express emotions. Musical experience can never be completely recaptured for a second time. So we should make every effort to give as perfect a performance as possible, for the bad lingers on in the memory as surely as the good. Just as good music helps to draw people into church, so will unworthy music, badly performed, turn people away from church, if only because it is negative and probably harmful.

Nor does music need to be difficult or elaborate to be automatically good. It is often the simplest music which has the greatest impact. These considerations will be as relevant in fifty years time as they have been for the past five hundred years. When all is said and done, the contemporary explosion of communication and knowledge provides the background for church music today.

Dom Augustine Morris, when Abbot of Nashdom, spoke of contemporary worship as emphasising 'modern words for modern man', a point worth considering.

We should explore any legitimate method which will encourage suitable new types of vocal and instrumental music in worship. Given the right situation and personnel, there is much to be said for the fusion of music, drama and, not least, liturgical dance. At its best, and used on occasion, it can be a valuable aid to worship but it needs to be superbly well done. It certainly has plenty of historical precedent.

The Revd Donald Reeves has made a revealing study of liturgical dance and drama, much of which was put into practice within the context of the services when he was Vicar of St Peter's, Morden.

Everything in the future, no less than in the past, will depend on people, each using their own talents. Doing this to the honour and glory of God is no mean occupation. But – and this is a big but – much will be jeopardised if we fail to communicate the vitality and joy which is the underlying ethos. This is a real danger. Our church services are often far too dull and for this the clergy must bear considerable blame. 'Poor old so-and-so' said a certain bishop I knew, 'he makes the Gospel sound the dullest news on earth'.

The Church of England contains within its ranks an extraordinary diversity, yet it can be very inflexible when it comes to the crunch. This applies both to the clergy and to the musicians and their music. Whether born of innate conservatism, or sheer cussedness, this can be detrimental and in the long run dangerous. We must be thankful that on balance the liturgical reshaping of recent years has done much to redress this tendency.

There must be a healthy regard for the best of all ages, and even healthier awareness for the best of today, of which there is much. A passing flirtation will not suffice.

The final word must be on the importance of music as a

necessary ingredient of complete worship. The angry parson may put forward his reasons against music, but the fact remains that well-performed and well-presented music is a proven aid to worship and something people desperately need. The power we musicians have is immense, though our full awareness of this is sometimes questionable in its application.

Surveying the complete spectrum as I see it, I would forecast a very fair outlook, provided we will it. It is a challenge we must meet, and how exciting if we view it aright.

And finally, a thought for us all:

> O Lord Jesu Christ, who hast created and redeemed me, and hast brought me hither where I am; thou knowest what thou wouldest do with me; do with me according to thy will, with mercy. Amen.

(A devout prayer of King Henry VI.)

Appendices

APPENDIX 1

Organists' salaries and fees

The Incorporated Society of Musicians, working in conjunction with a number of bodies including the RCO and the RSCM, have produced a comprehensive 14 page booklet called *Notes on Employment for Organists*. This contains a wealth of information for both professional and amateur church musicians and can be obtained from the RSCM at 35p including postage.

APPENDIX 2

Benefits of RSCM affiliation

Advice on any matter concerning church music, choirs and organs. Personal visits by staff members to choirs in their own churches. Courses ranging from a half-day to a week, at Addington or at local centres, for juniors or adults concerned with the ordering of music in worship. Festival services locally or regionally arranged. Literature, including the magazine *Church Music Quarterly*. Publications – musical and instructional – at low cost to members (many of them with a 50 per cent discount) and facilities for obtaining the music and books of any publisher. Choir badges and useful equipment for the choir. Special 'Chorister Training Scheme' for recruiting and encouraging young singers.

APPENDIX 3

Stop permutations

Correct use: 1 The right hand played an octave higher than written.

2 The use of single stops.

3 Playing without pedals or with an 8ft-flute as a relief from the prolonged use of 16ft-Bourdon tone.

4 Playing on uncoupled manuals.

5 Playing with the swell box either closed or open and avoiding the unmusical and indiscriminate 'pumping' which is frequently such a feature of organ playing.

6 Using families of stops rather than, for example, the mixing of flutes with strings.

7 The use of 8ft- and 2ft-tone provides a brightness less apparent when a 4ft- stop is drawn with them.

8 Using a 16ft-manual stop on its own but an octave higher.

Incorrect use: 1 The pedals constantly played an octave lower than written.

2 16ft-manual stops when playing *without pedals*.

3 If there is a Twelfth, using it without the Fifteenth.

4 Too much use of Mixtures. They can be hard on the ear.

APPENDIX 4

Hints on transposing

Remember how far you are going to transpose, then *think in the new key*. For example, a chord of C minor transposed up a tone becomes a chord of D minor. Each accidental needs to be worked out in its own right. In the end it is the ability to think and play in a new key while reading the printed music in another key.

APPENDIX 5

C. H. Trevor's seemingly endless capacity for finding simple organ music for every occasion has resulted in a large collection of books now available. These include:

Published by Oxford University Press:

Old English Organ Music for Manuals (6 volumes).

Seasonal Chorale Preludes for Manuals only.

    Vol. 1 Advent, Christmas, Epiphany, Lent, Passiontide, General.

    Vol. 2 Easter, Whitsun, Trinity, Festivals, General.

Two further volumes are published using pedals.

Organ Music for Services of Thanksgiving

Organ Book (6 volumes).

A Concise School of Trio playing for Organ.

A Concise School of Fugal playing for Organ.

Organ Music for Manuals (6 volumes).

Published by Elkin/Novello:

Wedding Album for Manuals.

Music for Funerals and Remembrance Services for Manuals.

Manual Miscellany for Organ—Volumes 1 and 2.

The Progressive Organist:

    Book 1 corresponding to Associated Board Grade 4

    Book 2 corresponding to Associated Board Grade 5

    Book 3 corresponding to Associated Board Grade 6

    Book 4 corresponding to Associated Board Grade 7

    Book 5 corresponding to Associated Board Grade 8

Volumes 6, 7 and 8 deal with all grades.

(The above lists represents a cross-section of what is being published in ever increasing quantities.)

APPENDIX 6

Faculties and certificates

Halsbury's *Ecclesiastical Law* (4th edition, 1975, paragraph 1312) states that 'Any works affecting the fabric or fixtures of a church will generally require a faculty or, where appropriate, an Archdeacon's certificate. This requirement will normally apply to any structural addition, alteration, demolition, renovation or repair, although in practice an exception is made in the case of minor current repairs.' This jurisdiction applies to the fabric and contents of all consecrated churches and such dedicated and licensed chapels as have been made subject to the faculty jurisdiction by order of the Bishop. Halsbury goes on to state that 'the repair or renovation of an organ is usually considered to require a faculty unless it amounts to no more than routine maintenance', but in practice the lines between what requires a faculty and what can be authorised by certificate are differently drawn in different dioceses. The certificate procedure has been abolished in several dioceses. Applications for faculties or certificates are made to the Diocesan Registry, but since all applications must be considered by the Diocesan Advisory Committee for the Care of Churches (DAC) it is advisable to consult the DAC informally at an early stage of planning. There are fees required by the Diocesan Registrar (and in the case of a faculty, the Chancellor) which must be paid, although in some dioceses such fees have been replaced by retainers paid to the Chancellor and Registrar from diocesan funds.

See also *A Handbook of Parish Property* by Kenneth J. T. Elphinstone (Mowbray, 1973), chapter 4.

APPENDIX 7

Hymnody

(An ideal way of keeping in touch with the subject is to join The Hymn Society of Great Britain and Ireland. The Secretary is The Revd Alan Luff, 7 Little Cloister, Westminster Abbey, London SW1P 3PL).

Suggested reading:

Erik Routley: Hymns and Human Life (historical) (John Murray).

Erik Routley: Hymns and the Faith (theological) (John Murray).

Erik Routley: The Music of Christian Hymnody (since the Reformation) (Independent Press).

Erik Routley: The English Carol (Herbert Jenkins).

Erik Routley: Hymns Today and Tomorrow (words) (Darton, Longman and Todd).

Dearmer and Jacob: Songs of Praise Discussed (OUP).

John Telford: The Methodist Hymn Book Illustrated in History and Experience (Epworth Press).

Parry and Routley: Companion to Congregational Praise (Independent Press).

Alan Dunstan: These are the Hymns (on choosing them) (SPCK).

Bernard Manning: The Hymns of Wesley and Watts (Epworth Press).

John E. Rattenbury: The Evangelical Doctrines of Charles
    Wesley's Hymns (Epworth Press).
John E. Rattenbury: The Eucharistic Hymns of John and
    Charles Wesley (Epworth Press).
G. F. S. Gray: Hymns and Worship (on words) (SPCK).
Norman Goldhawk: On Hymns and Hymn books (Epworth
    Press, 1979).
David W. Perry: Hymns and Tunes Indexed (Hymn Society
    and RSCM, 1980).
J. M. Barkley (ed): Handbook to the Church Hymnary.
    3rd Edition (OUP 1979).
Alan Dunstan: The Hymn Explosion (RSCM Handbook
    No. 6).
Ronald Jasper (introduction): A Hymn Guide for the Sunday
    themes of the New Lectionary (ASB), compiled by a
    York diocese group (Mowbray).

APPENDIX 8

General reading matter on Rite B (Series 1 and 2 Revised)

C. O. Buchanan: A Guide to Second Series Communion
    Service (Church Book Room Press).
This Do . . . A new version of 'Here we offer . . .' adjusted to
    the 1967 Liturgy by Denis E. Taylor (Religious Educa-
    tion Press).
E. C. R. Lamburn: Alternative Services—Using '1967'
    (Series 2) (W. Knott and Son).
Holy Communion Series 1 and 2 revised, with introduction
    and notes by William Purcell (Mowbray).

APPENDIX 9

*Published musical settings of Rite A (Series 3) Holy
Communion include*
(*Published with Congregational Card unison version)

Patrick Appleford: Mass of Five Melodies (Weinberger).

Patrick Appleford: New English Mass (Rite A) (Weinberger).

Peter Aston: Holy Communion Series 3* (RSCM).

Peter Aston: Seasonal Sentences (RSCM).

Reginald Barrett-Ayres (Novello).

David Butterfield: The St John's Setting of Series 3* (Grove Books).

Alan Dixon: The Walton Folk Eucharist (Mayhew-McCrimmon).

Christopher Dearnley and Allan Wicks: Published in three versions:
    Full Music (OUP).
    As part of Series 3 service book (AS 325), see page 93.
    Altar Edition (SPCK).

Christopher Dowie (OUP).

Martin Ellis (Banks).

Christopher Field: Mass of St Peter (Weinberger).

Joseph Gelineau (Ascherberg).

Alan Gibbs: St Margaret's Communion* (RSCM).

Jack Hawes* (RSCM).

Martin How: St Nicholas Service* (RSCM).

Martin How: Sanderstead Service (MD. Music Co).

Ian Hubbard* (Novello).

Ian Hubbard and Neil Cocking: Salisbury Setting (Mayhew-McCrimmon).

Peter Hurford* (Novello).

John Jordan: The Chelmsford Service (Mayhew-McCrimmon).

John Jordan: High Leigh Eucharist (Mayhew-McCrimmon).

Sister Mary Christine, CSMV (St Mary's Press, Wantage).

William Mathias* (OUP).

Missa de Angelis (St Mary's Press, Wantage).

Philip Moore (Addington Press – RSCM/Mowbray).

Dom Gregory Murray: A Unison Setting of Series 3 (Mayhew-McCrimmon).

Colin Nicholson: The Saint Botolph Service (Mayhew-McCrimmon).

Hayward Osborne* (Weinberger).

Anthony Piccolo: Canterbury Mass (OUP).

Charles Proctor: The Winchelsea Communion (Lengnick).

Betty Pulkingham: The King of Glory Setting (Celebration Services (Post Green) Ltd, 57 Dorchester Road, Lytchett Minster, Poole, Dorset BH16 6JE).

Brother Reginald SSF: The Saint Damian Eucharist (Mayhew-McCrimmon).

Keith Rhodes (Banks).

W. H. Rowe (Cramer).

John Rutter* (Novello).

Ian Sharpe: St Katherine's Service* (Stainer and Bell).

Martin Shaw: An Anglican Folk Mass* (adapted from the original version) (Curwen).

Richard Shephard: The Addington Service* (RSCM).

Richard Shephard: The Wiltshire Service* (RSCM).

Richard Shephard: Seasonal Sentences (RSCM).

Howard Stephens: The Osterley Service* (Roberton).

Philip Tomblings (Oecumuse).

Robert Walker* (Novello).

Arthur Wills: Missa in memoriam Benjamin Britten (Addington Press – RSCM/Mowbray).

Alan Wilson: Mass of All Saints* (Weinberger).

Alan Wilson: Mass of Light* (Weinberger).

APPENDIX 10

General reading matter on ASB (Rite A)

Many books, commentaries, pamphlets and articles have been written, and continue to appear. There are many omissions from this sample check list which nevertheless aims at being broadly comprehensive.

George Reindorp: Holy Communion Series 3 (Mowbray).

Paul Bradshaw: In rememberance of me (Mayhew-McCrimmon).

A Commentary on Series 3 (Liturgical Commission/SPCK).

The Presentation of the Eucharist (SPCK).

Colin Buchanan: Anglican Worship Today (Collins).

Michael Perry: Sharing in one bread (SPCK).

H. A. Lawrence Rice: To be a pilgrim.

Ronald Jasper: The Eucharist today (SPCK).

Ronald Jasper: All change (article) (Mowbray).

Michael Moreton: The Book of Common Prayer made fully perfect—A critique of Series 3 (The Church Union).

The Alternative Service Book 1980—a Commentary by The Liturgical Commission.

William Purcell: *A Communicant's Manual* with introduction and notes on the Holy Communion Rite A service (Mowbray).

Lionel Dakers: *Music and the Alternative Service Book* (Addington Press: RSCM/Mowbray).

David Austerberry: Celebrating the Liturgy (Mowbray).

Jean Mayland: Getting to know your ASB 1980 (Mowbray).

Grove Booklets on Ministry and Worship are an extensive and widely ranging series which is constantly being added to. Colin Buchanan, a member of the Liturgical Commission, is the go-ahead person responsible for these and other Grove Books published at Bramcote, Notts.

Series 3 material published by Grove Books includes:

Music for the Parish (Green and Ogilvie).

Series 3 for the Family.

The Language of Series 3 (David Frost).

A Guide to Series 3 and its Music (P. E. Dale).

Among the many articles on Series 3, two by Dr Ronald Jasper (former Chairman of the Liturgical Commission) are of special interest:

Holy Communion Series 3 (published in the April 1972 issue of *Church Music,* a Roman Catholic journal).

A sermon by Dr Jasper in Westminster Abbey was reprinted in *The Times* on Monday, October 4, 1971.

APPENDIX 11

Useful addresses and telephone numbers:

The Royal College of Organists, Kensington Gore, London, SW7 2QS (01-589 1765 or 581 2026).

The Associated Board of the Royal Schools of Music, 14 Bedford Square, London, WC1B 3JG (01-636 4478 or 636 9085).

Royal Academy of Music, Marylebone Road, London, NW1 5HT (01-935 5461).

Royal College of Music, Prince Consort Road, London, SW7 2BS (01-589 3643).

Trinity College of Music, 11 Mandeville Place, London, W1M 6AQ (01-935 5773).

Guildhall School of Music and Drama, John Carpenter Street, Victoria Embankment, London, EC4Y 0AR (01-353 7774).

Incorporated Association of Organists. Philip Brereton, 18 Duffins Close, Shawclough, Rochdale, Lancs. OL12 6XA.

Incorporated Society of Musicians. General Secretary, Miss Susan M. Alcock, 10 Stratford Place, London W1N 9AE.

National Federation of Music Societies, Francis House, Francis Street, London, SW1P 1DE (01-828 7320).

Organs Advisory Committee of the Council for Care of Churches, 83 London Wall, London, EC2M 5NA (01-638 0971/2).

Organ Advisory Group (Roman Catholic). Hon. Secretary, Mr John Rowntree, The Cottage, 2 Burys Bank, Greenham Common North, Newbury, Berks, RG15 8BZ.

Royal School of Church Music, Addington Palace, Croydon, CR9 5AD (01-654 7676/7).

Index